# Funny
# How Things
# Turn Out

# Funny
# How Things
# Turn Out

*Judith Bruce*

**SIMON &
SCHUSTER**

London · New York · Sydney · Toronto · New Delhi

A CBS COMPANY

First published in Great Britain by Simon & Schuster UK Ltd, 2012
This paperback edition published by Simon & Schuster UK Ltd, 2013
A CBS COMPANY

1 3 5 7 9 10 8 6 4 2

Simon & Schuster UK Ltd
1st Floor
222 Gray's Inn Road
London WC1X 8HB

www.simonandschuster.co.uk

Simon & Schuster Australia, Sydney
Simon & Schuster India, Delhi

A CIP catalogue record for this book is available
from the British Library.

ISBN: 978-0-85720-821-7
ISBN: 978-0-85720-822-4 (ebook)

Printed and bound by CPI Group (UK) Ltd, Croydon CR0 4YY

In loving memory of John William Bruce
November 1931–February 2011
and
John Richard Newmarch Miles
April 1933–July 2011

# Contents

## JUDITH'S STORY

THE END STORY

# Acknowledgements

I would like to thank Catherine Smith and Dr Celia Hunt of University of Sussex for their help and encouragement.

# PROLOGUE
## (2005)

# Never Have Me to Live With You

It's dark in this room. She is eating her dinner in twilight. Mummy. Over 100 years old. With final-stage macular degeneration.

Dinner is on a white plate with a plastic rim fixed around it so that she doesn't push the food off the plate onto the tray. She struggles with it in her armchair.

'What is it?'

'It's Cornish pasty, Muriel,' says the girl, as she disappears out of the room.

'*What* is it?'

'Cornish pasty, Mum.'

She can't see – the lamplight isn't bright enough. But if I put the centre light on it will be too much for her. Why do they just bang it down and assume she will be able to eat it?

'That's the Cornish pasty.' I point my finger at it. 'And over there are the potatoes – I think they're sautéed – and here are some peas and some fresh leeks – *not* frozen.'

'*What's* frozen?'

'Nothing's frozen. I said those were fresh leeks, *not* frozen – and there's some swede, in that corner.'

'Fresh what?'

'Oh never mind.'

I watch and remember the old days.

'*Never have me to live with you, dear ... put me in a home.*'

She always said it. '*When I'm old I don't want to be a nuisance to you. No one should spoil their lives looking after their ageing parent. It's wrong. No question.*'

I took her at her word. She lost her sight; she lost much of her hearing; she fell, broke a wrist and the shock upset her heart rhythm; she turned 100 and Social Services assessed her as needing full-time care.

So she is getting it. Here, in this converted farmhouse at the end of a narrow track off the trunk road to the Sussex coast. It is kind, it is caring – it is chaos. She wishes she wasn't here.

Her fork descends tremblingly into the centre of the mashed swede, coming down sideways and scooping up some gravy and some mince and pastry. This clings to the fork as it is carried towards her mouth, but falls back on the plate again. I think of those grab things in amusement arcades when I was a child. They always got hold of something you wanted and dropped it before you could have it.

'Try again, Mum.' I push some of the meat and potatoes onto the fork with my finger so that this time it sticks on.

'"If you get through that, you won't hurt,"' I murmur. 'As Nanny used to say.'

'Who used to say what?'

'Nanny. Father's mother. Used to live with us until you sent her packing to Auntie Winifred. She'd look at the food on the plates and say, "If you get through that you won't hurt."'

She lays the fork back in the gravy, turning her face towards me.

'I can't *see*,' she moans. 'I wish I could die, but I don't know how it's done. I worry about that.' She picks up the fork again.

'Some old people stop eating,' I say. 'So I've heard – and then they die.'

'Yes,' says my mother, capturing the last piece of pastry, 'I've heard about that too. I did try it, but I got so hungry, I had to give it up.'

'It's an awful way to die,' I say. 'Don't try it again.'

'Don't try what again?'

'Not eating.'

'Not what?'

'Oh *Mother*!'

'Well, wait till you're 102 – you might not hear so well either.'

She turns her attention back to her plate, struggling to find the mince.

She needs more light. I move her lamp nearer the edge of the table and notice the old, framed photographs standing beside her alarm clock. Why does she keep them? They clutter her space.

'I can't eat any more of this, dear.'

She has given up the fight. Eating is too difficult. Half of the food is left on the plate. I take her tray from her and put it on her chest of drawers, under the window.

'What is that view out there?' she asks, frowning.

'It's just the garden, Mum, and the patio outside the residents' lounge.'

'Just the what?'

'JUST THE GARDEN AND THE PATIO.'

'I don't like it. Draw the curtains. And don't *shout*. Keep your voice down.'

I draw the skimpy curtains against the fading light, and sit down in the visitor's chair again, next to her. We sit in silence, as she tries to dislodge the last pieces of food from under her false teeth with her tongue.

The old pictures sit in silence in the lamplight, with us. Flickering shadows when the lights are low.

Her mother, hair coiled on top of her head, gown, bustle, velvet trimmings, small hands clasped in front, standing beside an aspidistra; Mummy herself, aged five, in a frilled pinafore, short white socks, buttoned pumps, with a huge picture-book on a low table before her; her seven brothers and sisters sitting, standing, crawling all over a vast Edwardian chair; her brother Fred, in uniform; her beautiful sister Lucy aged nineteen; my father, with Brylcreemed hair, looking like Rudolph Valentino, standing next to Mother, a white cloud of wedding dress and bouquet (just her nose protruding) outside a church; and me, aged eight years on the back doorstep with my doll. And I remember it all. My memories, and hers, intermingled, since she never stopped talking to me about the past from the time I could stand.

'Why is there no photograph of your father, Mum?'

'Whose father? Your father?'

'No. I know what my father looked like. *Your* father.'

'*My* father? I don't know. But I was in awe of him. He lost interest in all of us after he'd spawned us.'

Once in the dear dead days beyond recall.

# MURIEL'S STORY

# The Walk With Father (1907)

She didn't want to go, but Father, all pipe and overcoat, bowler hat in hand, had said, 'Polly, get Baby ready for a walk. I shall take her with me this morning.'

It was a Sunday, cool and windy. A March day. She was four.

Her mother fussed round her, putting her into her best coat and hat.

'How lovely, darling. Father is going to take you for a walk. You will enjoy that, won't you? Now, come along, hurry up. Don't keep Father waiting. Have you got your gloves?'

She felt small, dressed up and terrified. She hardly knew her father.

Outside he walked briskly ahead of her.

'Keep up,' he called over his shoulder. 'We shall take the tram to Enfield.'

She recalled little of the tram journey. Of the walk, she remembered that the pussy-willow was out – twigs with furry pods. A sky bowled by clouds, moving ahead as fast as Father. And lambs racing against them in the fields. She remembered that her father took no notice of these things. And that she was glad when they got home, her cheeks roughed and buffed pink from the wind.

She knew she was born in 1903. In Highbury. A good address, though not as good as Islington, where her aunts lived.

She was the youngest of eight. As she was delivered Dr Barker asked Mother, 'How many children is that now, Mrs Newmarch?'

'Eight,' replied Mother.

'And how many are living?'

'All of them, of course,' her mother replied.

Kathleen, Fred, Lucy, Frank, Norah, Edith, Richard and now Muriel. They called her Baby. They called Edith, Mollie. They called Richard, Dick – or sometimes, 'Filthy Richard'. (It was a joke.) But all of them living, all of them healthy, all of them hungry and all of them in need of clothing. And educating.

Father was a bank clerk. A safe job, but he was not paid a lot. What did he think he was doing, having eight children? Not thinking at all, in fact. He wasn't interested – often failed to recognise them if he met them in the street.

He was a Victorian, from a good family, fallen on hard times. 'Reduced Gentlefolk' was the expression Mother used. Muriel knew her father was a gentleman. He just was. He had been brought up to think as a gentleman. It had nothing to do with money – which was good as there wasn't any.

Mother Kept Up Appearances on a small income, and hid their poverty from Father, who lived happily in a world of his own, where anything as vulgar as money was not an issue.

It was a noisy household. 139 Aberdeen Road. They had taught her the address.

Muriel and her brother Dick were the youngest. Then there were three older children – Norah, Edith and Frank; two teenagers – Fred and Lucy; and grown-up Kathleen, who had a job.

Kathleen. Kathleen would come home and throw the shoeboxes off the kitchen table when Muriel was playing dolls' houses with Dick. 'You kids, get all this rubbish out of the way and go and play somewhere else.'

She made you feel very small.

Then she *was* small.

It puts you at a disadvantage, being tiny. Everyone is taller and stronger than you. With a tiny voice as well, you never get a hearing. Not in a big family like hers. Not that they weren't nice to her (except for Kathleen, who wasn't nice to anybody).

If their parents went out in the evening, her brothers and sisters would play their favourite game: throwing Baby over the Banisters. Two of them would take her up to the top of the stairs, and three of them would stand at the bottom. Then she would be hurled from the landing into the arms of those below. And they never dropped her. She knew that they wouldn't.

At the back of the house was a garden. Nobody did any gardening; it was just a smooth patch of clay. She had a photograph taken out there once – sitting on Fred's lap on one of the kitchen chairs. He was almost grown-up then, in knickerbockers, boots and a check cap. She wore one of her frilled pinafores. The sun was out, and the clay looked shiny, like a pond.

She played with the cat on this patch. Taggy was his name, short for Taglioni, who was a horse. A Derby winner.

Taggy was the family cat, but she thought of him as hers. He always came trotting to her when he saw her. She was the one who cuddled him, she was the one who dangled a piece of rolled-up newspaper tied to a string over his head so that he could bat it about. When she was unhappy Taggy knew. He would jump onto her lap and put his paws round her neck so she could bury her face in his fur and smell his faintly fishy smell. If there was a stronger love than the love between her and Taggy, she didn't know what it was. Warm and comforting, and vibrating with throaty pleasure, he would secretly come to her bed at night.

That was if he wasn't out hunting. Which he often was after dark. When he was tired of this, in the early hours, he would sit outside the front door, from where he could reach the letter-box and the door-knocker. He would then lift the knocker up and down with his front paw, waking the household until someone came to let him in. But it had to be stopped, so Father found a way of tying the knocker down at night. With string. They had to laugh.

# Don't All Die (1908)

Muriel lay awake in the bed she shared with Norah. She was not only awake, but in tears.

It was the middle of the night. She could see the moon

where the bedroom curtains were slightly apart (they had to be apart so that some light came in – Muriel did not like to be in the pitch dark). And it was quiet. Deathly quiet. The only person in the world who was awake was Muriel Newmarch. The only person in the world who was worried out of her life was Muriel Newmarch.

Norah turned over, grunting. Muriel lay mouse-like, thinking and crying quietly.

Today had been a nice day – lovely and sunny, and Auntie Florrie had come to see them. Dear Auntie Florrie who was so dainty and pretty.

Auntie Florrie had worn a navy blue dress with a high frilled collar and a tight waist, and carried a cream lace parasol. She didn't like the sun.

'I can't stand the glare, dear,' she said to Mother. That had been this afternoon.

The clock downstairs in the hall struck three times. Muriel knew that meant it was three o'clock in the morning. A time when you should be asleep. But she was too worried.

She thought about Auntie Florrie's visit. They had had tea in the front room with an iced cake, bread and butter and strawberry jam and lemon curd tarts. And Florrie had brought Muriel a present. A little book with a picture of a rabbit in a blue jacket on the outside. She had explained that it was by someone called Beatrix Potter who wrote books for children and did all the drawings inside as well.

'Say thank you nicely, Baby,' said Mother. 'Say, "Thank you Auntie Florrie."' But Muriel flung her arms round her aunt and buried her face among her frills instead.

'I think that's a thank-you, Polly,' said Florrie to Mother, and smiled her smile.

'Put it somewhere safe, Moo,' said Mother. 'Don't get jam on it – we will read it together later.'

So Muriel had slid off her chair and gone into the dining room and put it on the table.

That was the nice part of the day.

She sat up in bed and looked at Norah beside her. She was lucky to be asleep, and not sitting up awake and worried.

Because it *could* happen. What she was worrying about. It could.

She leaned against her pillow and looked up at the shadowy plaster cornices on the ceiling. The moonlight gave them fantastical shapes which would be interesting, if she weren't so worried.

After Auntie Florrie had gone home, Muriel had run into the dining room and got her new book from the table. She had found Mother in the kitchen and put her arms round her knees, where her white apron hung, holding the little book in one hand.

'Mother! Mother!' she cried. 'Will you read to me, please? Will you read my new book to me?'

Her mother had bent and disengaged her arms, very gently.

'Not now, darling. I've got Father's supper to get – and then the washing to do. I can't read to you now. Later, darling. Later. Ask me again later.'

Muriel looked down at the tiled kitchen floor. 'You never have time. You're always too busy. You will *never* have time.'

Her mother put an arm round her shoulders. 'Well that's

how it is, Baby, when you've got a family and no help in the house. I have to do the shopping, do the cooking, do the washing, do the cleaning, feed everybody – I have to do *everything*. Heaven knows what would become of you all without me.'

'What *could* become of us?' asked Muriel. 'What do you mean?'

Her mother pulled her closer and bent and kissed the top of her head.

'Nothing, silly. With me to look after you all, make sure you don't get ill or into danger.'

She released Muriel, and straightened up, looking round at the cluttered sink.

'Now I must get on, darling. It's what mothers do.'

She walked across the kitchen. Muriel watched her go, the book still clutched in her hand.

'Have a glass of hot milk and go to bed, darling,' her mother said.

So that is what she had done. And now her Peter Rabbit book lay by her side of the bed, unread. She was starting at the Dame School next month, and she would learn to read there. But that was not till next month.

And there was all this worry to deal with. What would happen if Mother died and they had no one to look after them, feed them and keep them from danger? Then they would *all* die. But, worst of all, supposing the others died and left her behind, on her own?

She started sobbing hard.

Norah turned over, and opened her eyes. Then she struggled up in the bed until she was sitting, looking at Muriel.

'Moo!' she cried. 'Whatever is the matter with you?'

'I'm frightened,' sobbed Muriel.

'What of?' asked Norah, putting an arm round her.

'I'm-frightened-that-you-will-all-die-and-leave-me,' Muriel gabbled.

Norah's arm dropped from her shoulders. Her amazed face stared into Muriel's.

'You're frightened of *what*?'

'That-you'll-all-die-and-leave-me. Alone.'

'But there are SEVEN OF US! Nine, if you count Mother and Father. Why would we all die and leave you? It wouldn't happen. It isn't possible. Don't be silly. Don't make a disturbance about nothing. You woke me up, you stupid thing.'

Norah could be sharp when she was cross.

Muriel pulled a handkerchief out from under her pillow and blew her nose.

'Do you promise it won't happen?'

Norah had wriggled down in the bed again.

'Of course. Don't be a baby. Go to sleep and shut up.'

She humped over, turning her back.

Muriel slid down slowly, her handkerchief a wet ball in her hand. There were a lot of people in the family. It was true. But even so, people die and leave you. That was true as well.

She pushed the wet hankie back under her pillow. You never know what's round the corner. What you have to do is make the best of the little bit of life you have. She made up her mind she would do that – and fell asleep as the clock downstairs struck the half-hour.

# The Butcher's Dog (1911)

Sitting on the pavement was not comfortable. Even in your coat and hat and gloves it was chilly. And damp. Mother would be cross if she knew, but Mother was inside the butcher's shop getting the meat and Muriel needed to get down low. So she had slid down the wall outside the shop until she was in a sitting position, bringing her head level with that of the butcher's dog.

It was Saturday morning in Highbury. It was 1911 – Muriel knew that. She was eight and went to the Dame School where they taught you to know the date and your address and to speak French. The month was November and it was not at all warm. Skirts, button-boots, trousers and spats all swished past, and horse-drawn vehicles rumbled through the gutters. Saturdays were always busy. People shopping, meeting, talking.

But the best person to talk to was the dog as he sat outside the shop. He was a big dog, teddy-bear-coloured, rough-coated, with a studded black collar round his neck. His paws were enormous and hairy – hunter's paws. But his eyes were tender under his ginger eyebrows and his pink tongue lolled out as he turned his head towards her.

'What's your name, then?' asked Muriel.

The dog looked at her.

'You must have a name,' said Muriel. 'All dogs have a name.'

The dog held her gaze – then licked her face.

'Ugh,' said Muriel. 'That was wet.'

She stroked his head.

'Have you forgotten your name?' she asked him.

Damp was beginning to penetrate her coat and her flannel skirt. At school they sometimes grew mustard and cress on damp flannels. Her bottom felt like a mustard-and-cress patch now.

The peculiar butcher's shop smell of raw meat and sawdust wafted out from the open shop door. If she swivelled round and craned her neck she could just see Mother at the counter talking to Mr Harrison in his striped apron. Maybe she was buying a hare for Father's supper. Father loved jugged hare. It smelt good when it was cooking but it looked sinister hanging in the larder with a cup over its face to catch the blood. It hung there for days before it got put in the pot. Anyway, 'you children' were never allowed to eat it as it was Father's special. But perhaps she was getting sausages. That would be a treat.

The dog still was not replying. But his eyes were speaking to her. Or she thought they were. What does a dog think, she wondered. It was looking at her very intently. It must be thinking something.

Suddenly she glanced up. That reflex you have when someone is watching you. Not the dog this time. A boy. A boy, leaning against a lamp-post on the other side of the street. She knew him. He was nine. A year older than she was. Soppy Laurence Miles who was always reading a book. Yes. He'd got a book in his hands now. Leaning against a lamp-post, reading a book on a Saturday morning in Highbury. That was very soppy indeed.

He smiled at her. She did not smile back. She didn't smile at soppy boys. Anyway, she was much more interested in the butcher's dog.

Mother swirled out of the shop quite suddenly, her shopping bag bulging, her purse in her hand.

'Oh, Moo, whatever are you doing?' she cried. 'Sitting on the pavement in your coat and hat! What will people think?'

Muriel scrambled to her feet. 'I was talking to the dog, Mother.'

'Talking to the dog! I never heard such nonsense.'

She put her purse in her shopping bag and started vigorously brushing the back of Muriel's coat with her spare, gloved hand.

'Look what you've done. You've got mud all over the back of it. A good coat like that – how could you be so silly?'

'It's only Kathleen's, cut down.'

'Never mind that – it's very good material and we can't afford to be careless with clothes. You won't get a new one till goodness knows when.'

She stopped brushing and gave Muriel her hand.

'Come along. There's a lot to do today. We'll brush that coat again at home when it's dried out a bit.'

Muriel looked over her shoulder at the dog, as it stared after her.

'Goodbye whatever your name is,' she said. 'Talk to you again.'

'Not if you're with me, you won't,' said her mother.

'You'll never guess what,' said Muriel. 'I saw that soppy Laurence Miles on the other side of the street while you were in the shop. And he was staring at me.'

'I expect he was. Sitting on the pavement like that. Goodness knows what his family think of us all. I dread to think.'

Muriel thought how much more sensible animals were than people.

# Topsy (1912)

Muriel left the Dame School at half-past three every weekday and now she was on her way home, her linen schoolbag over her shoulder.

She was wearing a green velvet dress with a frilled white collar spread out over her shoulders that Mother had made her from one of her old coats. It had long sleeves and matching white cuffs and she was much too hot in it. It was her best dress, so she had worn it today because of The Photograph. She was also wearing white socks and black button shoes. And no coat – because the dress was warm enough.

It was a quarter to four, the cherry blossom was out on the trees that lined the road, the sun shone and Muriel was happy because it was now the Easter holidays. She was walking quickly as she wanted to get home to the tea and buns that she knew Mother would have ready. Her only time with Mother. When she could talk to her – before everybody else crowded in.

A cart was grinding along the road, some way behind her. She could hear its wheels and the clip-clop sound of a horse. It would be nice to talk to a horse, although she was not sure how you spoke to horses. Cat, as a language, she understood, and also Dog, but Horse was more difficult. But then he probably wouldn't want to stop and talk anyway.

An unearthly noise was joining the cartwheels and the hooves. A voice. Crying out, 'AG-BONE! AG-BONE! AG-BONE!'

It was ghostly, this call. Wailing all round the villas and front gardens by which she was walking, over the chimney-tops and into the sky, mixing with the smoke from the chimneys, echoing and dying. 'AG-BONE! AG-BONE!' She knew that cry well.

Muriel stopped by the kerb, so that she could see him pass. The old rag-and-bone man, and his nodding horse with the jingling bridle. She could see them coming, slowly along the avenue. The rag-and-bone man always moved slowly, in case he missed someone coming out from a house with an old mattress or a battered chair that he could pile on his cart.

'AG-BONE! AG-BONE!' He sounded haunted.

She watched him as he approached, his horse clopping patiently as he held its bridle. And a lady in a pinafore came out of Number 14 with a dented tin bath in her arms.

Man, horse and cart drew to a scraping halt, and the rag-and-bone man took the bath from the lady. Much obliged, Mum — something like that he said, but Muriel couldn't hear. He chucked the bath on top of the wobbly pile of goods on his cart, touched his cap, got hold of the horse's bridle and moved on.

Muriel looked at the horse going past her as she stood on

the kerb. He had brass plates on his eyes – 'blinkers' they called them – and he looked thin. She hoped the rag-and-bone man was kind to him. If he wasn't, Muriel would find him and hit him. Nothing was worse than being unkind to animals. She had once attacked a man she had seen beating a dog on Highgate Hill – kicking his shins until Mother had had to apologise and pull her away. The man was pretty surprised though. Probably he was nicer to his dog after that.

Muriel walked along behind the horse and cart until they turned off down Winton Road on the left. Only a few hundred yards more and she would be home. She could tell Mother all about her day and The Photograph.

The man with the camera had come in at half-past eleven, as they had been told he would. They all sat up straight at their desks, though Muriel reckoned she sat straighter than any of them. Mother had put a green satin ribbon in her hair, with a bow just above her ear, so she hoped she looked nice – and the white collar spreading over her shoulders was pretty. Looking at Freda Parrington next to her, with her spindly hair and her serge frock with ugly buttons down it, she thought she must look better than her, anyway. So she sat up straight, while Freda slumped, looking cross. And Miss Jones and Mrs Bussell stood at the back of the room in their skirts and high-necked blouses, wearing strict faces.

The man had stood behind the camera, holding up a light, and FLASH, it went. They had to sit very still. But he seemed pleased when he left.

'AG-BONE! AG-BONE!' The rag-and-bone man's cry was fainter now. Even more creepy.

She crossed over the road, gaining the kerb the other side,

still thinking about The Photograph. Henry, the tabby from Number 25, jumped off his garden wall in front of her and wove round her legs, quivering for a few moments.

'Who's a lovely boy, then?' she said to him.

Henry's whiskery face looked into hers. He thought human beings meant food. She squatted down and stroked his head and his ears, because he liked that – then remembered her best dress and how it would be picking up the dust, so she stood up again quickly.

Time to get home. Because apart from The Photograph there was another thing to tell Mother.

In her schoolbag was her exercise book with 'Muriel Newmarch; Class 2; Composition' written on a sticky label on the front. As well as a new book, bound in maroon with a coloured picture on the front. Not on a separate wrapper, but actually on the front of the book. It had the title in gold letters above this picture: 'Us And Our Donkey' it said. The picture was of three children standing round a small grey animal. The donkey.

She was looking forward to reading this. But even better, inside the book, pasted opposite the title-page was a label with a decorative border in silver and the words 'Prize – Awarded to Muriel Newmarch for Composition – April 1912' in swirly letters. And the 'Muriel Newmarch' bit was written in blue-black ink in Mrs Bussell's writing.

She had reached her front gate: the shabbiest one in the street. No one had time to paint front gates – or front doors, or window-frames – in her house. And no one weeded the front garden either. But she didn't look at these things. This was Home.

She ran down the side-way and round to the kitchen door at the back, which was always open. She knew her mother would be there, making tea.

Rushing in, she thumped her schoolbag on the big kitchen table and said, 'Mother, Mother, I've got such a lot to tell you!'

Her mother moved from the stove to the table, with a teapot in her hand.

'Wash your hands first, Moo,' she said. 'Before you start eating buns and talking.'

Muriel dashed to the kitchen sink and dabbled her hands under the tap. Then she came back to the table and sat on one of the wooden chairs. She undid her bag and put the two books in front of her mother, as she sat down, pulling a jug of milk towards her to put in the teacups.

'I won a prize, Mother,' said Muriel. 'For my composition.' She opened her exercise book.

'Look – this is it, Mother. What I won the prize for. It's about Topsy, the Circus Horse.'

'Well done, Moo,' said her mother, getting up from the table. 'I must look at it later.'

'Oh look at it now, Mother. Please,' said Muriel, pushing it in front of her.

She reached for a bun from the plate in the middle of the table and started stretching for the butter.

'It's not very long, Mother. Or I can read it to you.'

Her mother picked up her cup of tea from the table and moved away with it.

'I just haven't got time now, Baby,' she said. 'I've got pota- toes to peel. Father's bringing a visitor home tonight.'

She put her cup of tea down on the draining board, and picked up a potato from the colander in the sink.

The front door banged.

'And now Kathleen's home so none of us will get any peace,' said Mother.

'But it's only just half-past four, Mother!'

'She had a half-day at the office,' said Mother, 'I'm afraid.'

Muriel looked at her composition on the table in front of her. She was proud of it. It had such a good beginning: *Crack went the whip, and Topsy jumped through the hoop for the third time* ... And she had written it. All of it. And got a prize.

'What's Baby doing taking up the table with her rubbish?' said Kathleen, coming into the kitchen. 'Clear it up. Get rid of it.'

Muriel stuffed the books back into her schoolbag.

'Where's my tea, Mother?' asked Kathleen.

'Coming, dear,' said Mother.

'AG-BONE! AG-BONE!' called the rag-and-bone man, distantly.

# April (1913)

April Summer. That was her name. Muriel thought it was the prettiest name she had ever heard. April. So much better than Muriel.

Everything about April was better, nicer and more desirable. April had lovely hair – blonde and curly, not mousy and straight like her own – and deep green eyes and beautiful long legs. Not bandy, like she feared hers were.

Better than that, April was her best friend.

They were standing outside the Summers' front gate in Maple Close, just round the corner from Aberdeen Road, both wearing cotton dresses with a pinafore over. It was after tea, but still hot. If you touched the paint on the Summers' front gate it burned you. Muriel tried it, and took her hand away quickly.

April was teaching her how to dance. April went to dancing lessons – something Muriel's family could not afford. But the dancing just went with April's glamour. Her starriness. You would expect someone like April to have dancing lessons, but you wouldn't expect Muriel to have them. And April didn't. Expect Muriel to have them. She didn't expect Muriel to have anything much. So she could tell her friend what was what. Things Muriel needed to know about. And, especially, she could teach her how to dance.

'You go like this, Moo,' she said, balancing on one leg.

Muriel copied her, raising her right leg.

April started circling her foot, her knee raised.

'Rond-de-jambe and rond-de-jambe,' cried April.

Muriel circled her foot obediently.

'Rond-de-jambe and rond-de-jambe, a glisset hop and down,' said April, circling the leg, doing a little jump and bringing her two feet together in first position.

'Not like that,' she said as Muriel staggered slightly. 'Do it properly. Look. I'll show you again.'

The evening sun shone, and two little girls, one fair and one dark, hopped on one leg, pirouetted and balanced and stood with feet in first position to the chant, 'Rond-de-jambe and rond-de-jambe, rond-de-jambe and rond-de-jambe, glisset hop and down . . .'

Next door's dog came to watch, and sat at a discreet distance on the pavement a few feet away.

'That's better, Moo,' said April. 'Now do it again.'

Muriel hopped and twirled obediently, as April called out 'Rond-de-jambe and rond-de-jambe, glisset hop and down . . .'

'What does it mean?' asked Muriel breathlessly, as she came to a stop.

'It's French,' said April. 'All ballet is in French. That's what ballet is. It's French. Don't you know French?'

'I know *bon-jour* and *comment-allez-vous* but not these words,' said Muriel.

'Your mother should send you to dancing classes,' said April, pulling a slipping ribbon out of her hair and tying it on again. 'You should know how to dance and how to speak French so that you can attract men. My mother says.'

'Why?'

'It's important. For when you are older. You need to look pretty and wear pretty clothes. And dance. Then you get the best man.'

'What do you mean – the best man?'

Next door's dog got to its feet, and looked at them.

'Don't you know *anything*?' asked April.

Next door's dog pattered over to Muriel and sniffed her hand. She bent and patted him.

'I do,' said Muriel, straightening up. 'I know men and women get together and girls should look pretty so that men like them – but what is the *best* man?'

'The one with the most money, of course,' said April. 'The one who can buy you the most things.'

'Don't you need to like him, though?' asked Muriel.

'Not at all,' said April. 'That doesn't matter. My mother said.'

The Summers' front door opened, and Mrs Summer put her head out.

'April,' she called. 'Come in now. It's getting late. Say goodbye to Muriel.'

'I've got to go in, Moo,' said April. 'But I'll see you tomorrow, won't I?'

'Come to tea with us tomorrow, Muriel,' said Mrs Summer, coming down the front path and opening the gate. 'I've bought a Battenberg cake.'

Bought cake! They could afford bought cake *on weekdays*!

So of course she said yes please. She loved Battenberg cake – the marzipan outside and the pastel checks inside. And the jam. She wasn't sure if she loved Mrs Summer, though. There was something about her. Something hard. Not like her own sweet mother.

'Four o'clock, then, Muriel. Tomorrow,' said Mrs Summer, shepherding April indoors with her.

'Thank you,' said Muriel, as they went in.

She stooped to pat the dog again, and started the short walk home.

The thing about April was, she knew *absolutely everything*.

# The Bank in Shoreditch (1915)

A Victorian building in Shoreditch High Street – standing four-square to the pavement – built to inspire confidence in its stability and power. The Westminster and Provincial Bank.

Above it, two floors of cavernous rooms, large enough to house a family of ten. And this was home now. For all of them. The rooms echoed with family quarrels and laughter. In the bank below, father worked as chief cashier. You had to be a gentleman to work in a bank. Father was content.

How on earth had they ended up here?

Muriel was sitting at the sash-window of the top-floor room she shared with her sister Norah. She was wearing one of Norah's dresses, cut down to fit, with a small collar added. The sun streamed in, which she didn't like. Heatwaves made her feel faint and she hoped this wasn't going to be one. She missed Aberdeen Road. She missed April. She even missed Mrs Bussell and Miss Johnson.

But Father had come to the end of the line. He spent all his money, thinking he was a man of means. Men from his background should be able to afford a comfortable life. It was his right. She knew that was how he thought.

Unpaid bills. In Aberdeen Road there had been a kitchen cupboard with a hook inside the door on which these were hung. A huge bunch of them, clipped together. Occasionally her mother opened this door, unhooked the bills, looked through them, put them back, then sat on a chair with her apron thrown over her head, rocking back and forth.

As Muriel was the youngest, tiny and pale-faced, she used to be sent to the butcher for the meat because her mother didn't dare face him. Mr Harrison couldn't demand his money with menaces from such an appealing little girl – that was the thinking behind it. Father was flabbergasted. 'What are you worried about, Polly? He's only a *tradesman*!'

So things had got bad. Then they got worse and the bank had to be informed about his precarious financial position. They agreed to pay all his debts for him if he took the next vacant position they had to offer. Which was here, in the East End of London.

Below, in the street, was the jellied eel stall. The smell was all-pervasive, particularly if the wind was in the wrong direction. Opposite was the Gents public toilet, of which the same could be said.

She had never eaten jellied eels. Mother said they were common. They never said 'toilet' or 'pardon' because that was common too. 'Housemaid's English'. Not that they had a housemaid, as they could never afford it. Her mother was still doing all the work and got very tired.

She herself had been uprooted from the Dame School and sent to the Central Foundation School for Girls in the City.

When they first went there, her mother said to the principal, 'Such a pity there are so many Jews in this area,' and the principal had become very angry and replied, 'My Jewish girls are the cream of the intellect at this school.' And after that she didn't seem to like Muriel very much. She found herself in the Disobedience Room frequently and sank to the bottom of the class. And there was no doubt that the Jewish girls were cleverer than she was. She came to hate school. It was huge and she felt overwhelmed. She had one friend, who was also tiny – Milly Gallitsky. Milly was all right, but she kept pulling at her arm saying, 'Listen, *listen* – I want to tell you something . . .' Sometimes she said, 'Muriel, have you never eaten Blue Soup? You must try Blue Soup, Muriel. My mother will make you Blue Soup.' It sounded foreign and not at all safe. Not like English food.

Perhaps if she was taller life might be easier? Or if she had been born a boy? Boys seemed to have a better time. When she asked Father why she hadn't been born a boy he said, 'They didn't have enough putty,' and went back to his newspaper.

And now there was a war on. The War to End All Wars. They hoped it would be. The one to end all wars. No one needed another war like this one.

London's East End was bombed regularly. When she got home from school at half-past four she feared she would find that the bank had been hit, and her mother, father and brothers and sisters all killed. Her two eldest brothers were at the Front. Most young men were dying. Would Fred and Frank die with them?

She could be sure of nothing. Anxiety became a habit with her.

# Mollie and Lucy Get Home Late (1916)

It was a hot night. Too hot to sleep. London was still, sweaty and stuffy. Not a breath of air, no cooling breeze. Awful. Just what she hated.

Muriel perched on the window-ledge of the top-floor bedroom. Top floors got hotter than floors lower down, she had noticed. Why did she have to be at the top of the building, when she hated the heat so much?

She was in her nightie, with her hair plaited in a rope over her shoulder. Norah was in bed asleep. She could see her motionless body under the counterpane if she turned her head over her right shoulder. Snoring gently, Norah was. As usual. Why did Norah not find the heat in their bedroom intolerable?

She turned back to look down at the street below. Empty, except for a pair of drunken men rolling out of the Gentlemen's toilet opposite – holding each other up as they went, singing their rollicking song.

*Mabel dear, listen here, I'm afraid to go home in the dark . . .*

One of the men stopped, leant his arm against the brick wall of the pub at the corner of the street, and vomited into the gutter.

Muriel immediately felt sick. Seeing other people being sick always made her feel sick too. It was horrible, anyway.

Vomiting in the street like that. But it didn't seem to bother the drunk, who reeled away from the wall, put his arm round his friend's neck again and continued, round the corner, singing lustily.

*Every day, the papers say — there's a robbery in the park —*
*I'll sit alone in the YMCA, singing just like a lark —*
*There's no plashe like home*
*But I will not go home in the dark . . .*

It was quite a popular song at the moment. She liked these music hall songs. Her favourite was 'Oh, Oh Antonio!' That was a good one. She sang it quietly to herself as the drunks staggered out of sight along the side street and their song faded into the distance.

*Oh, oh, Antonio, he's gone away,*
*Left me alone-io, all on my own-io,*
*I'd like to meet him, with his new sweetheart —*
*Then UP would go Antonio and his ICE-CREAM CART!*

You had to sing that last line with a lot of emphasis, as that was where the joke was.

She tilted her head slightly and saw a crescent moon in a velvet sky. Like a jewelled brooch in a box. Not a full moon yet, which was good. You don't want the Bomber's Moon. Not with a war on.

Norah stirred in her sleep, and Muriel slid off the window-ledge and tiptoed over to her. She stood, looking down on her, and Norah's eyes half opened.

'What you doing, Moo?' she murmured.

'Waiting for Mollie and Lucy,' whispered Muriel.

'Wait for ever if you wait for them,' said Norah sleepily. 'Why not come back to bed?'

'I'm too hot,' said Muriel. 'I don't know how you can sleep.'

'Mmm—' mumbled Norah, turning over again. 'You're too fussy to live.'

'Think I'll die young, then?' asked Muriel.

'No,' said Norah, dropping off to sleep again. 'Only the good die young.'

Muriel tiptoed back to the window-ledge, and leant on it, pushing her head out under the open sash – breathing in the hot, stale air.

She heard laughter in the distance. Girlish laughter. Mollie and Lucy's laughter. And footsteps. They were on their way home, but they were in the next street. It would take five minutes to get to the bank from there, if you went all round the houses.

But Mollie and Lucy never went all round the houses.

Leaning further out of the window, Muriel looked down, fixing her eyes on the exit to the Gentlemen's lavatory.

She could hear her sisters' conversation now. She could just pick out words.

'He said –' (Giggling.) 'No, listen – he said, "My mother told me you wouldn't like me if I wasn't wearing my uniform."'

'And you didn't, did you?' (More giggling.)

Then silence. Not even the sound of footsteps.

Muriel craned out of the window, straining her ears. There

was a burst of laughter from the pub, as a group of people pushed open the doors and came out onto the pavement. She heard them walking off, talking noisily.

Then footsteps started echoing. And girlish laughter again.

And there they were. Her sisters, in their high heels and lightweight dresses, arm in arm, coming up the steps of the Gents lav. Their shortcut. They always took it.

Mollie and Lucy. Happy and silly.

'Lu, you're too good to live, you are,' Muriel heard Mollie saying, as she hugged her sister's arm.

'I know – I shall die young,' giggled Lucy.

A gale of laughter swept them as they reached the pavement.

They shouldn't walk through the Gents like that. Asking for trouble, Muriel thought.

She got off the window-ledge, and crept back into bed. Perhaps it was getting a little cooler? It had to get cooler, didn't it? It must be getting on for eleven o'clock.

Down below she heard the heavy front door bang, and then the light steps of her sisters as they came up the stairs.

She pulled the coarse linen sheet up to her chin, kicking the counterpane off on her side, and put her head on the pillow, looking at the ceiling. She could feel with her feet the seam down the middle of the sheet where Mother had turned it 'sides to middle'.

Maybe when she was older she would take the shortcut home, too. But she didn't think so. It didn't seem at all safe to her.

You couldn't be sure of anything in this life.

# Lucy (1917)

It was gloomy in the flat above the bank. Although there were many tall sash-windows, there were also a lot of trees and buildings outside and the light didn't get through always. Certainly not at this time of year. So it was dark. And quiet.

Muriel sat at the wooden kitchen table, her head on her folded arms, her face turned to one side so that she could breathe better. Breathing was a problem when you were trying not to cry.

This was where the family ate in the evening. Mother and Muriel's brothers and sisters. Father had his dinner on his own – always something specially cooked by Mother. Frank and Fred were still away at the Front, but Kathleen, Norah, Mollie, Dick, Muriel and Lucy sat here. Lucy was the most beautiful. Also the nicest, the sweetest, the wisest of all her sisters.

Rain started hitting the kitchen windows, softly, but persistently. She raised her head and watched the rivulets running down the panes as her tears dribbled down her cheeks.

This time last year she had sat in this kitchen with Lucy. 'You know what, Baby?' Lucy had said. 'Love is a funny thing.'

Lucy was twenty years old. Muriel was thirteen.

'Is it, Lu?' Muriel had said, not knowing what this was all about.

'Yes,' Lucy had said, putting an arm round her. 'Sometimes

you think you've got it and then suddenly you find that you haven't got it after all.'

'Oh,' Muriel had said.

Lucy had given her a squeeze. 'Don't forget that,' she had said.

Now she was fourteen Muriel thought she knew what that conversation had been about. At the time, Lucy had been engaged to an officer who was fighting in the war. She wore an opal ring which Muriel admired and coveted. Everyone thought she was happy. But she had said that funny thing about love and Muriel wondered if Lucy had met Another. That sort of thing happens. Muriel had read about it. But Bert had come back from the Front unexpectedly, on special leave, so that he could marry the lovely Lucy and they had got married quickly. All the time her sister had not been cruel enough to tell him that she didn't love him any more. Probably. But Muriel could never be sure.

When her Bert went back to the Front after a week's honeymoon he left Lucy pregnant. Which was nice, and Lucy had been pleased about it. Then again – had she?

A wind began rattling the windows. There was a wedge somewhere that you could jam in between the frame and the sash, but Muriel didn't know where it was. Someone had put it somewhere, no doubt, but everyone had more important things to think about than rattling windows.

Because Lucy was upstairs in bed. Muriel had sat with her and she had looked as if she was about to speak to her. So Muriel had taken her hand, but it was as cold as a chicken from the larder. And as still. Lucy was never going to speak again.

She had the baby upstairs, in her own bedroom. The birth had been OK, although she had made a lot of noise. But you do. If you are having a baby. It was a boy. Colin she called him. Then she had said to Mother, 'I didn't like that doctor. His hands were dirty and he had blood on his jacket.'

He was an old doctor. All the good young doctors were still at the Front with the troops.

Lucy got ill a few days afterwards and now, a week later, she was speechless, unsmiling and dead. From puerperal fever. Blood poisoning. It should never have happened. They were living in the twentieth century not the nineteenth. People knew about disinfectant nowadays.

It was a waste. A waste of her beloved sister. She had been twenty-one years old. And sweet. And good. She used to say, 'Ah well, the good die young.'

She couldn't possibly have known, though. Surely?

Yesterday, Lucy's husband had come and taken Colin away and no one knew where they had gone. And this morning Mother and Father were at the undertaker's.

Muriel leant her head on her arms again. Her tears slipped round her face and fell into her ears. Some dropped onto the table. The doors rattled, the windows shook. Her shoulders shook. Her life shook. The world was dark. There was no joy. There was no certainty. There was no God. There was no kind mother-rabbit in an apron who could put you to bed and give you comforting medicine from a huge spoon. It was all a lie.

The Aberdeen Road childish days had vanished and instead there was poverty, worry, sadness and death. Especially death. Muriel had become anxious and pessimistic. She feared the worst by nature.

# Father's Not Coming Back (1920)

'Polly, Polly – don't let them take me.'

Her father was on a stretcher and he was weeping. Two men were trying to carry him through the rear door of the bank to a waiting ambulance.

Muriel was seventeen, standing uncertainly in the dark lobby with her mother. She had never seen her father cry. Father had always inspired her with awe. Life revolved around his wishes but he had been a distant figure – never a working part of the family machine.

'Sh – don't disturb your father' or 'Your father's having his supper – don't bother him' or 'Don't worry Father – Father is not to be upset' were the words most frequently uttered by her mother all through her childhood. Father had always held sway.

Once he had brought a friend from the bank home for supper. Afterwards he had said, 'My daughter, Edith, will now entertain you on the pianoforte.' Muriel remembered her sister's surprised face (apart from the fact that everyone called her Mollie as she hated 'Edith', she could not play the piano).

Mother saved the situation. 'Don't be an idiot,' she had hissed at him. 'Mollie has never learnt to play.'

'Nonsense, Polly, my dear,' Father had replied. '*All* young ladies play the pianoforte.'

'Well, *our* young ladies don't.'

'But why not?'

'Because we can't afford to pay for piano lessons,' Mother had said. Then, 'Do you know my youngest daughter, Muriel?', changing the subject and pushing Muriel forward to meet the visitor.

They had all laughed about it afterwards, although Father had never understood why.

But he had been a Presence. Father. Someone to be tiptoed round, someone not to be confronted or argued with. Someone whose place in the family was pre-eminent. And what was happening to him now?

He was very ill. Muriel knew that. She had seen him grow-ing thinner and looking sallow over the last few months. But this was awful. He was clutching Mother's hands, howling uncontrollably. He was shaking with terror. He was not behaving like a gentleman.

'I don't want to go, Polly!' he cried. 'Not there, Polly! Not there! Please not there!'

'Shhh, darling,' her mother said, bending over him and kissing his forehead. 'I will come and see you this afternoon. I promise I will come.'

The men raised the stretcher and took it through the open door. Muriel heard her father's frantic screams as he looked at her mother for reassurance. But her lips were pursed together like bent twigs. It was bad.

The door slammed and the engine of the ambulance splut-tered into life.

'Where are they taking Father, Mother?' she asked.

'Shh, darling,' said her mother again. 'He has to go to the hospital in Muswell Hill.'

'When will he come back?'

'He won't, darling. He will never come back. It is the place for Incurables. Father has cancer.' She put her arms round Muriel and wept.

Father was going to die, then.

Another one.

First Lucy and now Father.

It was a dark place, the flat over the bank.

# The Boyfriend (1921)

Muriel was going to her first dance. With a young man.

She was in the kitchen, with a roll of material on the kitchen table. Beside it lay a large pair of scissors and Mother's sewing basket.

For a job like this you had to get close to your work, so Muriel was kneeling on top of the table, among all the slithery satin, with three or four pins in her mouth, trying to fold her length of material in half.

The kitchen door was open and outside she could see the familiar muddy patch. It was clay, of course. That was why it was smooth and shiny. And no one had done any gardening yet. But it was good to be back in Aberdeen Road after all the sadnesses of Shoreditch. Good that the war was over and Frank and Fred had returned – although Frank had been gassed and they didn't like the sound of his chest.

It could not be said that she missed Father – but she grieved for Lucy. None of them would ever get over that. No one would call a child Lucy and no one would wear opals again in her family.

She knelt back on her heels, surveying the pale blue sea of slippery material (a bargain in Berwick Market last week), and picked up the scissors, cradling them with her other hand in front of her. Thinking. Where would you put the first cut?

The fashionable outline for dresses now was easy. You just had to cut out two straight sides and a little bit of sleeve – then straight across for the neckline. You sewed the two sides together, and added a belt, or a sash, round your middle, just above your hips, and, as her brother Dick would say, 'Robert is your mother's brother . . .'

Of course you needed to neaten the seams and make sure the hem was at the right length – just below the knee. But that was easy. It was the cutting part that might be tricky.

She had better buck up as she would not have the kitchen to herself for much longer.

Taggy wandered in from the garden. He looked old and scruffy. He had something wrong with one of his eyes, which was gluey. He didn't look cuddly any more. But he sat, tail curled round, looking at her, as if he would like to jump up onto the table with her.

'Shoo – go away, Taggy,' she said. The last thing she wanted on the blue satin was his muddy paw marks.

The old grandfather clock in the hall struck four. Four o'clock on a Saturday afternoon and they would all be back by five.

She had to grasp the nettle. It was like cutting her fringe –

that had taken courage and a lot of guesswork, but it had come out all right.

Taggy wandered away, discouraged.

She bent over the cloth, and holding the material with her left hand made the first crunching cut in her blue satin. Once started it seemed inevitable that she must continue – *scrunch, scrunch* – scissors moving inexorably forward and up to where she estimated she should start curving in for the sleeve, then out again, and then across in a straight line.

She paused there, and knelt back on her haunches. Laying the scissors down on the table, she removed a pin from her mouth and applied it to the two raw edges she had created. Then another pin and another until one side was pinned together.

A pot of stock that Mother had on the stove gave a sudden bubbling noise, and she looked up. But it was all right. It wasn't boiling over.

She looked down at her work again. How would you make both sides the same?

Well, you would fold it together, sides to middle, and cut the other side against the pattern of the first. That was obvious.

It wasn't easy – the satin was so difficult to hold onto. But it had to be done, so she managed to fold the loose part underneath what she had cut, and stuck a few more pins down the middle.

It would be her first grown-up dance, and this pale blue satin dress her first dance dress. She would wear it with a string of Mother's pearls and her new slave bangle, pushed right up her arm to the fat part above the elbow.

She liked Tom. She was glad he had invited her to the dance. He was always smiling and charming, and he rode a motorbike with a lot of shiny bits. She didn't think she would introduce him to April – although she wasn't sure why she wouldn't.

Yes she was.

*Scrunch, scrunch* – her scissors went along the uncut side, matching perfectly with the other half.

But the trouble with Tom was his religion.

*Scrunch, scrunch* – the confident sound of the scissors made her feel everything would turn out right, though.

The pot on the stove began to boil over.

'Bother,' said Muriel, and laid her scissors down on the blue satin, scrambling off the table and going to the stove to remove the saucepan. It had been boiling long enough anyway.

She stood the pan on the draining board, and returned to the table. Really the cutting part was finished. She reached for Mother's pin-cushion, extracted more pins to put in her mouth and, pin by pin, pinned the other side of her dress together. Then she picked the whole thing up from the table and held it at arms' length.

It wasn't bad. It was just a bit lopsided, but that wouldn't matter as hems and dresses could be asymmetrical nowadays. It was a lovely colour and would go with her eyes, which were her best feature. Not many people had grey eyes. Eyes, good, legs not good. That was the truth. But even her legs would pass muster with her high-heeled grey leather shoes and a pair of silk stockings. And the pearls. And the bangle. And she would make a sash to tie round.

She laid the pinned dress over her arm to take upstairs.

Tomorrow she would borrow Mother's sewing-machine to finish it.

But there was this problem with Tom. He was a Roman Catholic. Did that matter?

She stood, with the blue satin over her arm, the scissors in her hand, looking down at the remnants of material on the table, wondering. They didn't have anything to do with Roman Catholics in her family. No Popery. Church of England only – always had been.

Would Mother mind?

Muriel thought probably she would.

She went upstairs with her dress and the scissors. She would enjoy next Saturday evening with Tom. She would ask him why he had to be a Roman Catholic and couldn't he change? Why not?

She had never been to a dance before, she had never ridden on a motorbike – and she had never kept a secret from April before either.

## The Interview (1922)

What to wear. That was the question. Muriel was making herself another dress (after the success of the blue satin one), but it still had pins in it and seams and hems to be finished. It would take her another two days.

And the interview was today. The interview for her first job as a newly qualified shorthand-typist. Her secretarial skills had been learnt at Clarke's College, as Mother would not let her attend Pitman's. Pitman's was common. Her shorthand was Pitman's (not Gregg's), but otherwise she was untouched by the Pitman's culture – which she knew was not for ladies.

She had a pair of silk stockings and her grey shoes, with a strap over the instep and a button fastening, slightly pointed toes and a small heel. Very fashionable. But you can't go to an interview in shoes and stockings. You have to put something on top.

Standing in the middle of the bedroom she shared with Norah, in her underwear, staring at a shaft of sunlight as it hit the rug, her hands on her hips, she knew her brain was getting nowhere – and the clock downstairs was striking eleven. Only an hour before she had to be at the offices of Savill & Sons, Land Agents. A half-hour bus ride away.

She opened the door of the wardrobe and peered inside. On the right hung Norah's clothes – smart and suitable for the businesswoman Norah had become. On the left was Muriel's girlish collection of cut-downs and home-made dresses and blouses. She went through them hopelessly and then looked at the new coat hanging on the right. Norah had bought it last week and not yet worn it. Muriel had watched her unpack it from its Swan & Edgar's bag and hang it in the cupboard. She had thought it was lovely then. A beautiful silky material, an understated beige colour. And a fashionable cut.

Cautiously she took the coat off its hanger, swung the wardrobe door shut, closing it with her foot, and slipped the coat on. She turned and looked at herself in the long mirror on the front of the wardrobe door.

A perfect fit. Looked marvellous with her shoes. All she needed was a hat and bag – and she had those.

But she still had the problem of what to wear underneath. Only she didn't, did she? Because if she buttoned up the coat, no one would know she only had her slip and knickers on. So the problem was solved.

Downstairs the clock struck the quarter. Now she was in a rush. She grabbed her hat from the bedside chair and crammed it on – it was the sort politely called a 'cloche', impolitely called a 'po' – so it showed only the fringe of hair she had cut herself across her brows. She had once tried folding her hair up with pins and a velvet band to create the fashionable short bob look, but it had been a failure. Muriel had therefore resorted to Mother's sewing scissors and done the job that way.

Pulling on her gloves, she took another look at herself in the mirror.

Even in high heels it had to be said that she was tiny. She was eighteen now, so she supposed she would never grow any taller. But with the hat and the gloves and the bag – and especially the coat – she no longer looked childish. That was something. She looked like a real 1920s businessgirl. It was a pity her legs were bandy. Not as bandy as Norah's, but more bandy than Mollie's. That was Father's fault. They had his legs.

Time to go. She ran down the stairs and let herself out of the front door.

'Muriel – where are you going?' called her mother from the kitchen.

'Out,' said Muriel as she ran down the path. 'To that interview I told you about.'

'When will you be back?' said her mother.

But Muriel had gone.

An hour and a half later the bus rumbled back to Highbury
through the roads lined with London plane trees, with Muriel
aboard. She would be home for a late lunch. She looked at the
respectable houses and the neat front gardens as she rode by.
And thought again how nice it was to be back in Highbury
after living in Shoreditch. In fact, the only good thing about
Father's death had been that the bank had given Mother a
good pension and helped them buy the house.

She thought about her interview. It had gone well. She had
met an elderly gentleman with a twinkle and a beard, who
looked like the King and certainly behaved like him. A courtly
person. And a younger man, who was his son, with the same
twinkle. So handsome. Muriel was in love.

And they had both been nice to her. She had enjoyed talking to them. They seemed to like her and she certainly liked
them.

She peered out of the bus windows. Nearly home. A pity
it had started to rain and she had brought no umbrella – but
then she wasn't wearing a dress either. What was the Boy
Scout motto? 'Be Prepared'. Well, she wasn't.

Yes. They had liked her. No question.

'We'd like to offer you the job. Can you start now? We
really need someone.'

'Er,' Muriel had hesitated.

'You can hang your hat and coat on the pegs and begin

straight away, as far as we are concerned.' They indicated the coatstand and an empty desk, upon which stood a typewriter under a cover.

'Let me help you,' said the young man, as she stood up. He put his hands on the shoulders of Norah's coat. Helpful. Polite. But.

They might be surprised if she took it off. .

'Oh that would never do. I have to go home and tell my mother. She will wonder where I've got to.' That was good – quick thinking.

'Of course,' said the elderly gentleman kindly. 'Lidell, what are we thinking of? Miss Newmarch must go home first.'

He smiled at her.

'We will see you tomorrow morning at nine, Miss Newmarch. Let Lidell show you out.'

And he did – and he looked at her as he opened the door for her. As if he was taking in her grey eyes. Her best feature. And as if he was not noticing the bandy legs.

What an escape! Supposing they had succeeded in getting her coat off her? There would have been nowhere to hide.

She rang the bell, and skipped off the bus as it stopped, running along the road to the front gate to avoid getting Norah's coat wet. Ladies don't run, she remembered her mother saying. This lady did.

Lidell, she thought. She had never met anyone called Lidell before. It was a lovely name.

She pushed the front gate and used her key to open the front door.

'How did you get on?' her mother called out from the kitchen. She came out into the hall, wiping her hands on her apron.

'All right,' said Muriel. 'I got the job. I start tomorrow.'

She needed to run up the stairs before her mother saw her.

'Muriel – you're wearing Norah's new coat,' cried her mother. 'What *are* you thinking of?'

'She won't mind, Mother,' said Muriel. 'She's always buying clothes and not wearing them. Anyway, she's not going to find out.'

'Who will you be working for?' called her mother after her retreating back.

'Someone called Lidell Savill.'

'Not Jewish, then,' said her mother, going back to the kitchen. 'That's something. A good old English family name. Nearly as old as Newmarch.'


# The Grass-Mower (1922)


Muriel had typed her first letter for Sir Arthur. And not made any errors, so there were no messy rubbings out or overtypings. The sheet came out of the machine clean and perfect. She laid it on the desk beside her while she found an envelope, wound it into the machine and carefully typed the address:

The Rt. Hon. Lord Farlane of McFarlane, MP
Kirkuldie House
Fifeshire

The office was quiet today. Her friend Vera was away with a bad cold, which was in some ways a relief, because Vera had the thing they call 'BO'. Not that anyone said it aloud. It was whispered behind hands, and the men used to say, 'Don't the months come round quickly?' to each other when they passed her.

Muriel thought that was unkind, because Vera couldn't help it. Vera had clean hands and shiny, washed hair. And she was always well dressed. It wasn't a personal hygiene problem. Perhaps Vera should go to a doctor?

A fire crackled in the grate beside her. It was only October, but the weather had got chilly and wet, so she was glad of the warmth.

She looked at the letter again, and checked it with the shorthand notes in her spiral-bound book.

*Dear Lord Farlane,*
  *With reference to our letter of the 13th ult, we write to confirm our agreement with regard to the Kirkuldie Estate and with particular reference to the . . .*

One of Sir Arthur's sons blew in through the street door. The wind banged the door shut behind him, as he unfurled his umbrella and then started opening and closing it again, shaking it rapidly to get rid of the raindrops.

Sir Arthur had many sons working with him. This was Lidell. Muriel's favourite.

Lidell unwound the cashmere scarf from his neck, shrugging off his overcoat and hanging it on the coatstand. The umbrella went in the place for umbrellas below.

'Good morning, Miss Newmarch.' He was very breezy. Like the weather. 'You look extremely pretty, proud and pleased today,' he went on. 'Are you happy in your work?'

'Yes, thank you,' she said. 'Only my second week here and I took down a letter for Sir Arthur this morning, because Vera is away.'

Lidell held his nose. 'For dis relief much danks,' he said, through his fingers.

'Don't. She can't help it, you know.'

'All right. I won't. But only because you say so.'

He came and stood behind her, looking at the letter.

'That's a lovely, neat piece of work,' he said. 'And no spelling mistakes, as far as I can see. The Old Man will be pleased with you. Well done.'

Muriel didn't make spelling mistakes. Words mattered. She never needed to look anything up in the office dictionary.

'He gave me three more to do,' she said. 'But this is the longest one. All about an estate in Scotland.'

'Yes – old Farlane of McFarlane. Silly buffer,' said Lidell, going towards his office.

'He sounds rather grand.'

'Grand?' said Lidell, his hand on the brass knob of his office door. 'He's a daft old drunk. No one's grand, Muriel – everyone's human. All made of the same stuff, as t'were.'

Lidell went into his office and closed the door behind him.

Muriel put a fresh sheet of paper into her typewriter, winding it in until the gold letterheading 'Savill & Sons' was just two inches above the platen, as she always did.

*Dear Sir Geoffrey*, she clattered.

The tea-boy brought the tea, and the post. The clock

ticked. The fire crackled. A motor car rattled past in the street outside.

At 12.30 Muriel got up from her typing chair, put Sir Arthur's four letters neatly into a manila folder, each with its addressed envelope, and walked upstairs to his large office on the first floor.

She knocked on the door, and waited. She could hear Sir Arthur talking on the telephone inside. He was also harrumphing and coughing as if he had a cold. Perhaps he had caught Vera's?

She heard the click and the ting of the telephone being replaced, and knocked again.

'Come in,' he called.

Muriel opened the door and walked across the maroon carpet towards the polished oak desk at which Sir Arthur sat, like a captain on the quarterdeck, surrounded by polished brass – desk calendars, pen and ink trays, reading lamps and blotters.

Rain spattered the bay window behind him, and he was blowing his nose on a large white handkerchief.

'I've brought you the letters for signature, Sir Arthur,' she said, as she put the folder in front of him.

'Thank you, my dear,' he said, stuffing his handkerchief back into his top pocket. 'Most efficient. I can see you are going to become an office treasure.'

He was such a nice man. Kind and fatherly. Muriel smiled at him.

'Would it be all right if I took my lunch hour now, Sir Arthur?'

'Of course. Take more than an hour if you like. We're not

clock-watchers here.' Warmth shone from his face and his
plump body exuded goodwill. Benign. That was the word for
him. He made her feel happy.

'Thank you,' she said and turned, walking back across the
deep pile carpet in her high-heeled shoes to the door.

Going down the stairs she thought she heard another 'harrumph' from behind her.

She made for her coat and her cloche hat, hanging on the
stand next to Lidell's scarf and overcoat. And heard another
'harrumph' from upstairs. This time it was followed by gales
of laughter. Unmistakable mirth. Sir Arthur's office door
opened, and she heard his heavy tread on the stairs.

'Muriel, Muriel, my dear girl,' he said, as he came down,
one hand on the banister, the other holding a sheet of paper.
His face was rosy and tears were running down his cheeks.
What on earth was the matter?

Lidell had come out of his office at the commotion.

Sir Arthur held up Muriel's beautifully typed letter to Lord
Farlane of McFarlane. He seemed to be unable to breathe.

'Dear girl,' he managed between roars of laughter, 'what
do you think we were writing to Lord Farlane about?'

'Well, the estate, Sir Arthur.' Muriel was perplexed, but she
held her ground.

'With particular reference to what, my dear?' he heaved.

'Er – well, whatever it says there,' she said.

'What it says here is, *with particular reference to the grass-
mower . . .*'

Lidell started rocking backwards and forwards with
laughter. Sir Arthur mopped his brow with his big handkerchief. Muriel stood, on her high heels (you need these

if you are barely five feet tall), looking from one to the other.

'Should I have typed *lawn-mower*? In my notes it looked like *grass-mower*.'

Father and son collapsed on each other's shoulders.

'*Grouse-moor*, Muriel, *grouse-moor*,' groaned Sir Arthur. 'This is a Scottish country estate with a *grouse-moor*.'

'I've never heard of such a thing,' said Muriel. 'But I have now, of course,' she added. 'Should I retype it for you?'

He nodded. 'I think you'd better,' he said, turning and going back up the stairs, still mopping his shining face.

Lidell stood looking at her. 'Muriel, you are a card,' he said. 'Would you like to be our office *enfant terrible*?'

# Lunch With Lidell (1923)

Muriel was walking very fast downhill in high-heeled shoes, passing the front gardens with their hydrangeas and privet hedges, passing the row of shops – Mr Harrison's the butcher, Pavey's the grocer's – crossing over Pymm's Brook – *tap tap tappetty tap* – all the way to Brownlow Road. To see Dr Barker.

She needed to see him as there was certainly something wrong with her legs.

She looked down at them as she walked and saw her silk

stockings and bow-tied shoes moving in and out below the hem of her short coat, *tap, tap, tap*. Her legs were fine for walking with, and her feet and ankles were good – she had a nice high instep and well-turned ankles (whatever that meant). But they looked all wrong. *Tap, tap, tap, tappetty tap*.

A bus rattled past her, throwing up dust from the road. It was a dry, warm June day. Not exactly sunny as there was quite a lot of cloud. But you would call it a nice sort of day. Well, you would if you weren't upset.

But she *was* upset.

A man and a woman passed her, arm in arm. Quite elderly – possibly as old as fifty, or even more. He had a newspaper under his arm and a watch-chain across his middle, and his wife (Muriel supposed she was his wife) wore a light-weight cream cotton coat, belted round the middle. They smiled at her as they went by, and of course she smiled back. It was only polite.

But she did not feel like smiling. Not at all.

They would probably have noticed her legs. She always tried to make sure the sun was not behind her if she was walking along the street – otherwise they showed up really badly. But the sun wasn't out today. Anyway, wherever the light was coming from, it was surely in the wrong position and the fact that her legs were short and not absolutely straight would have been blindingly obvious. No question.

Of course, it was her face he had liked. He hadn't noticed the legs.

*Tap, tap, tap*. Only five minutes more and she would be at the doctor's. He would tell her the truth. Dr Barker had brought her into the world, and all her brothers and sisters.

What was more, his father had been there at the birth of her mother. He was their family doctor and absolutely to be trusted in all things medical.

And it had started so well with Lidell.

She consulted her small gold wristwatch on its black moiré silk strap. Five past three. She had made the appointment for three o'clock and she would be on time as she always kept her watch ten minutes fast in order never to be late for anything.

'Muriel, I'd like us to have lunch together some day this week; would you do me that honour?' That's what Lidell had said. Her heart had nearly leapt out of her mouth. But she'd replied steadily and politely. 'How nice,' she had said – a phrase she had heard her mother use on social occasions. 'How nice – I would be free on Wednesday.'

He wouldn't have known how flustered she felt. She had been the very model of decorum.

'Then Wednesday it shall be,' he had replied, with his sparky smile. Or did she mean 'sparkly'? It was both.

*Tap, tap, tap*. Nearly there.

Oh, the trouble she had taken with her clothes and her hair. She had snipped a little bit more off her fringe with the nail scissors so that her nice eyebrows and her grey eyes showed up to advantage. She had altered an old dress of Kathleen's – in a shade of pale blue that suited her – and she had splashed out on new shoes – three-and-eleven they had cost. She hadn't dared tell Mother.

Now Dr Barker's brass plate, standing in the middle of his holly hedge, appeared on her left. To the right of it was the green front-garden gate. She had arrived.

She leant over and clicked the latch with her gloved hand, pushing the gate with her knee as she went, so that it swung open. *Tap, tap, tap*, up the crazy-paved path to the steps to the front door. She pressed the bell and waited.

Ten minutes later Muriel was standing on Dr Barker's desk in his consulting room, upright in her coat, silk stockings and high heels. Dr Barker himself was on all fours crawling round the desk, looking up at her legs as he went round.

'Mmm,' he said thoughtfully.

Muriel looked down at him.

'Well?' she said. 'What do you think?'

'Just a minute,' he said. Then he began to crawl around the desk again, in the opposite direction, still looking at her legs.

'Yes,' he said. Then he got up.

'Let me help you down, Muriel,' he said, offering her his hand.

Using his swivel chair, she got down off the desk.

'Sit down,' he said, and indicated the armchair, set at an angle to his desk. He himself settled his comfortable bulk into the swivel chair, clasped his hands and put his elbows on the desk, looking at her with one eyebrow raised.

'What do you think?' asked Muriel. 'Are my legs very misshapen? Could something be done? Could they perhaps be tied together at night to straighten them while I sleep?'

Dr Barker made a snorting noise into his hands, and then looked up at her.

'I think,' he began, '*I* think you've got very nice legs. I don't think there is anything the matter with them at all.' He pushed the chair back and stood up. 'Now go home and stop having ridiculous notions.'

The consultation was over.

What could she say? She couldn't tell him about Lidell.

'Please send your bill to Mother,' was the grown-up thing and so that is what she said, as she got to the door of his consulting room.

'I don't think we'll worry about this one,' he replied, as he held the door open for her, his face wreathed in smiles.

She wondered if she had said something funny.

As she walked down his front path the sun came out from behind a cloud. It felt uncomfortably hot as she retraced her steps along Brownlow Road, over the brook and up the hill again. Still thinking.

If there was nothing wrong with her legs, then what *was* it? She had done nothing wrong during their lunch, had she?

They had gone to a smart expensive restaurant and Lidell had ordered a bottle of wine, but she had explained that she never drank wine. He had ordered her lobster thermidor but she had explained that she only liked plain food and could she have plaice and sauté potatoes, please? And he had said something about how he found her very fascinating and would she like to meet him for dinner and the theatre and maybe stay at the Ritz with him? So she had to explain that her mother wouldn't like her staying out late and not coming home at night.

What could have been wrong? She had behaved impeccably.

But the next day Lidell had hardly spoken to her – and the

day after that he had been almost rude. And now he never looked at her – well, not in the way he used to look at her last week.

When she had told April about it she had just said, 'Well, what do you expect?' What did that mean?

It was getting too hot as she tapped her way up the hill. The sun was on her back – in quite the wrong position – and her dress and coat were sticking to her. She was moist and miserable.

And the worst thing was that yesterday there had been a very smart woman waiting in the reception lobby at the office for Lidell at half-past twelve, and he had come down and whisked her off on his arm saying, 'I thought the Café Royal would be nice today,' and she had said, 'Lovely!' and looked really happy. And neither of them had noticed that she, Muriel, was standing there, with her notebook in her hand waiting to take a letter from Sir Arthur. Standing there. Watching them go.

So if it wasn't her legs – what was it? Was it something so dreadful that no man would like her?

*Tap, tap, tap.* She could see the black dog that sat outside the house at the top of the hill now. He was always there at teatime. Nearly home, where she would do some serious thinking.

Perhaps she had better agree to let Laurence Miles take her to a concert, after all? He was a bit quiet, but he was the right height and he made her laugh. And she quite liked music, so long as it wasn't noisy.

He wasn't dashing like Lidell. But he dressed well and he was fairly good-looking. And he liked her. And whatever it was that was seriously wrong with her, Laurence Miles hadn't noticed it.

She was nearly twenty now. Perhaps she should start thinking about her future?

## Tea in the Garden (1924)

It was a perfect afternoon. July – and she would be twenty-one in a week's time.

Muriel was walking slowly along Whittington Road in beige silk stockings and high-heeled shoes, wearing a plain navy dress with a cream collar and short sleeves, edged with the same material as the collar. Home-made, of course. She was getting rather good at running up dresses – although she also liked shopping in the West End. The little Jewish shops in Soho, where the fat lady owners stood outside trying to entice you in. But usually she couldn't afford what they had to sell so it was good she could sew.

The sun was very hot. In fact, it was her least favourite sort of weather. On the other hand, it was nice to have a birthday at this time of year, rather than when it was wet and cold. No question. And if you walked slowly like this, you avoided getting too sweaty. It would never do to arrive with her dress sticking to her back, or dark wet patches under her arms. (She had made sure to apply her O-Dor-O-No before she left home.)

A pigeon landed on the pavement in front of her and walked jerkily across to the kerb, searching for crumbs. A motor car rolled by, disturbing the gravel on the road, which was loosening because the tar was melting in the heat.

The pigeon launched itself into the air.

Muriel went on walking slowly, putting one neat foot in front of the other. She quite liked the look of her feet in their smart shoes. She had a high instep, which meant heels and a strap and button across suited her. High insteps were a sign of good breeding, Mother said.

She was going to tea at Laurence Miles's house. He had invited her last week and had offered to call for her and walk her over. But she had said, no, there's no need, good heavens, you only live round the corner. And after all, she had known the Miles children since she was six years old. Although, funnily enough, she had never met Mrs Miles – or Mr Miles, come to that.

Next turning right it was. Their road. Number 25.

She turned the corner and looked at her watch. Nearly half-past. Perfect timing.

The front gardens looked pretty. People had time to look after them, no doubt. Lupins, hollyhocks and antirrhinums rioted under window-ledges, and a buddleia was hanging over a front wall. Beautiful. High summer. If only it wasn't quite so hot.

She paused to look at a butterfly, settled on a front gate, moving its wings up and down – and wondered why it did that. Was it sunning itself?

Laurence would know. Laurence knew a great deal. She used to think he was soppy, but he wasn't. He was clever. He had matriculated at fifteen years old with a 'Distinction' in every subject. And his sister was clever too.

Muriel moved away from the butterfly, and wished she hadn't remembered Laurence's sister. Winnie. Five years older than him, six years older than she was. When they were children and Muriel was only five, Laurence's big sister had snatched her teddy-bear away from her and held it over a bonfire, saying she was going to drop it into the flames. Muriel had cried and in the end she had got her teddy back. But she didn't like Laurence's sister. You don't get over things like that. And you don't do things like that to a little girl unless you are a nasty person.

Muriel hoped his sister was not going to be there for tea.

She walked up the path and knocked at the front door, noticing how bright and polished the knocker was. And the front step blindingly white and scrubbed. They did things properly here. No question.

The front door opened and a very smiley large lady stood in the hall saying, 'Hello, dear. Do come in. So nice to see you, Muriel. And what a lovely day we've got, don't you think? Come in, come in, don't stand there.'

Laurence's mother. She was so nice. Warm and welcoming and talkative. Tallish, with her hair in a grey bun, wearing a silk dress and a long string of beads.

'Laurence,' she called over her shoulder as Muriel stepped into the narrow hall. 'Muriel's here!'

'So punctual you are, Muriel,' she beamed, and took her hand. 'They're all out in the garden – come on through.'

She led her along the hall, through the kitchen and out of the back door into a small garden, where a table was laid under a lilac tree. A white cloth, and matching plates, cups and saucers, every sort of cake including an iced coffee sponge with walnuts on it which was one of Muriel's favourites, bread and butter and a huge pot of home-made strawberry jam.

And there was Laurence, in his open-necked shirt, getting up and coming over to greet her, and a smallish, elderly man in glasses getting up out of a deck-chair.

'This is my husband, Muriel,' said Laurence's mother. 'Charley, come and say hello to Muriel. My goodness, dear,' she said, turning to her, 'we've known your family all these years but we've never met you before, have we? We know your sisters, of course, and your dear mother . . .'

Oh Laurence's mother was truly friendly. And his father came over and shook her hand and they sat down to the magnificent tea.

'Did you make all these beautiful cakes?' asked Muriel.

'I love baking,' said Mrs Miles. 'It's never any trouble. And Charley's got a sweet tooth, haven't you, dear?' She looked at her husband across the table and smiled. He smiled back.

'I've got a sweet tooth for anything you have to offer, Betty,' he said.

They were so jolly. Muriel felt happy with these friendly people. And Laurence's sister wasn't there. Winnie Miles made her feel small and stupid. It wasn't because of the teddy-bear. Winnie Miles was just like that. Anyway, she wasn't there, which made Muriel even more happy.

It was funny the way Laurence didn't speak to his mother, though. But he didn't say much, as a rule. He was a quiet person. Probably because he was clever. She would ask him about the butterfly in a minute. He would be bound to know.

But his mother was chattering away. She was telling her some story about their window-cleaner and how she had seen him from inside the house making funny faces through the window and it wasn't until he took his comb out of his pocket and started to comb his hair that she had realised he was using the window as a mirror and peering at himself, not making faces at her at all. She was amused by this story and two pink spots stood out on her cheeks as she laughed. She looked really pretty when she laughed and Charley sat and looked at her admiringly while she entertained. No one else got a chance to speak, but then, Mrs Miles was so amusing that no one else needed to say much.

Muriel loved her. Someone who talked.

Laurence leant back in his chair and lit a cigarette. The sun shone down on the cake crumbs and the plates with blobs of sticky strawberry jam left on the side. A wasp buzzed hopefully round.

'More tea, dear?' asked Mrs Miles.

'Can I help you, Mrs Miles?' asked Muriel, half getting up out of her chair.

'No, my dear, you stay there, I'll just put the kettle on indoors and come out and top up the pot for us all. And why don't you call me "Mother Miles"? It's more friendly, with you and Laurence getting on so well.'

And so it had gone. Lively talk, warmth, kindness, and endless food. Tea in the garden had become supper in the dining room, with cold ham and trifle, before Muriel went home.

Such hospitality. Quiet Laurence Miles had more to offer than she had thought. A really nice family and a lovely mother.

It was just a pity about his sister.

# Mother's Been Taken to Hospital (1925)

It was as bad as it could be.

Muriel was walking with her sisters down the hospital corridor – scrubbed tiled walls, echoing passages, nurses with triangular white caps, some with bonnets, all with aprons, scurrying to and fro, and the smell of disinfectant all around. The sun was slanting through the windows above, showing up the dust as it hung in the air.

The three sisters wore business outfits, cloche hats and gloves. They looked at one another with anxious faces, but said nothing – high heels echoing as they walked.

It had been an ordinary day. Just the usual. You woke up, you drew the curtains back, saw that the sun was out, washed, dressed, ate breakfast, hardly noticing Mother labouring with the big teapot and the bread knife, and scooted out of the front door to work. As always.

Muriel remembered going into the office, taking off her scarf, hat and coat, hanging them on the coatstand, putting her leather gloves in the top drawer of her desk for safety, and settling down to work. That meant taking the heavy cover off her typewriter, saying hello to Vera at the desk next to her, and getting her shorthand notebook out of the second drawer down.

'How did you get on with Laurence?' Vera had asked. 'At the concert?'

Vera was smiling, looking happy. Better than that, the awful

BO had disappeared. She had gone to a doctor, and then to a specialist, and they had found she had a decaying and putrefying tubercular bone in her nose. Poor Vera. But they had treated her, and here she was with her puff of dark hair held back by a bow, and her wide kind face beaming.

So Muriel had told her that the concert at the Albert Hall had been fine but it had been so hot that she had nearly fainted and Laurence had made her put her head between her knees.

'So he's quite nice to be with, then?' Vera had said.

'Yes – very nice. Very nice indeed.' Which was true, although whether he was more than that she couldn't tell.

She had smiled at Vera and wondered, not for the first time, why she did not get her hair cut into a fashionable bob. Then she had set to work transcribing a letter she had in her notebook from the night before.

So just an ordinary morning. Until eleven o'clock. Muriel remembered it was eleven o'clock because the tea-boy had been round, and the ornamental hands of the big office clock were at five past because the office clock was five minutes fast.

She heard the telephone ring upstairs in Sir Arthur's office, and she heard him answering it. She could discern a rough grumbling as he talked, but nothing more. He always talked like that on the telephone anyway. She heard the receiver go down. Then there was a noise like furniture being moved, Sir Arthur's door opening and then another door opening and a scrambling on the stairs.

Sir Arthur's son Rupert came running down, two steps at a time, looking strange.

'Muriel – Father would like to see you. Right away,' was what he said – and then he stood there looking as if someone had set light to the back of his coat, moving from foot to foot. Uncomfortably.

'Don't bother to take a notepad,' he added, as she picked it up.

Mystified, she had climbed the stairs, with Rupert following her and Vera gazing up as she went, eyebrows drawn together in a puzzled frown.

Rupert had stood aside for her as she entered Sir Arthur's office, and gone in with her, closing the door behind him. Sir Arthur was pacing up and down. He looked at her as the door closed. Rupert stood like a sentry in front of it, hands behind his back, legs apart.

The atmosphere in the room was odd. What was happening?

Sir Arthur came towards her and took one of her hands. 'Muriel, dear girl,' he said, 'you must go home. Immediately.'

'Good heavens, why?' She turned to look at both of them.

Sir Arthur dropped her hand and took his handkerchief out of his top pocket, mopping his brow. He suffered from overheating at times of emotion.

'Your mother has been taken ill, Muriel,' he said.

'Ill? How ill? What sort of ill?' she asked.

'Very ill, I'm afraid, Muriel,' said Rupert. 'They have taken her to the hospital on Highgate Hill.'

After that the morning had become quite different. Frightening and rushed. Rupert had got his car out of the office garage and driven her to the hospital, although she had hardly noticed the journey. All she had noticed was the feeling that the top half of her body was separated from the bottom half and in the middle was a great chasm. A void. She did not know what to think – it was better not to think – but if she didn't think there was nothing to fill that void. She felt suspended above it, fearing to fall into it.

And now, here they were, she and Mollie and Norah, walking along the hospital corridors to meet the doctor who would know what was wrong with Mother. It was serious, but how? Why? Mother had been just as she usually was that morning. Hadn't she?

A nursing sister was coming towards them.

'Are you enquiring about Mrs Newmarch?' she asked.

They stopped and said they were, and she indicated a bench against one of the tiled walls, on which they were to sit and wait. They sat in a line, as she walked away.

'Oh, Mol,' said Muriel to the sister next to her. 'Oh, Moo,' said Mollie. Norah said nothing. She was always the least communicative of the three of them. She stared ahead crossly. It was her way of hiding her feelings.

And so they stayed, on the bench, until the doctor appeared, wearing a white coat and a concerned expression. He sat with them and explained.

Their mother had collapsed outside the front door, on her way to do her shopping. Collapsed with an internal haemorrhage. A perforated ulcer. Gastric ulcers sometimes perforate and bleed profusely and dangerously with no warning. It was lucky that a neighbour had seen her lying on the front path and summoned the ambulance. They were doing all they could here now. They were going to have to operate. Meanwhile, it would be a matter of waiting. Waiting to see. He was sorry – sorry not to be more encouraging. The indications were not very good. But please wait. Would they like a cup of tea?

They sat and they waited, in their coats and their hats and their gloves, in the echoing hospital corridor, until the sun had dipped and the lights had been switched on.

When they saw the doctor coming towards them again, they knew. They knew from his walk, from his hands clasped in front of him, from his shoulders. From his face. Serious and tight.

He did not need to tell them. But he told them. Mother had not come round from the anaesthetic. They had done all they could. These things happened sometimes. Mother was dead. He was sorry. Would they like to see her?

Mother was dead. And she had never had time to talk to her. Not properly.

Muriel fell into the void.

# Under a Tree (1926)

It was sensible of Laurence to bring the black-and-white check rug to sit on. But Muriel wished that she wasn't wearing her black-and-white check cotton frock. It was perfect for today's hot July weather – short sleeves, lovely and cool. But Laurence had taken her photograph and she would be seen against the black-and-white looking like a matching table napkin. No question.

And she wasn't sure about her white straw hat either.

She peered into the shopping basket lying beside her. 'Do you want some more?'

Laurence was sprawled a few feet away, leaning on one elbow, in his open-necked shirt and sports jacket, grey-flannelled legs extended in the grass. The camera was on the ground in front of him. He was wearing a checked, flat, peaked cap. The latest fashion.

'No, thank you. I've had an excellent sufficiency.' He stared into the middle distance, looking across Grovelands Park Lake, ahead, under the trees.

Muriel pulled the basket onto her lap and burrowed inside it, bringing out two packets of sandwiches wrapped in greaseproof paper and two slices of home-made Victoria sponge in flowered paper serviettes, which she put on the grass between them.

'But your mother's made all this!' she cried. 'There's' – she paused, unwrapping the greaseproof packages and looking at the contents – 'ham sandwiches, tongue sandwiches, chicken sandwiches.' She lifted the corner of the paper napkins. 'Oh, and some sponge cake, here.'

It was ridiculous. They had already eaten four rolls and half a pound of cheese between them, plus a tomato each and an apple, and she was sure there was a pork pie still at the bottom of the basket.

Laurence turned to look at her. 'Put it this way – I have eaten as much as will do me any good.'

He was droll, her young man. Certainly unusual.

His eyes took her in for a moment. 'I like the hat,' he said, turning back to stare at the lake.

Muriel pulled her sun hat off her head and laid it on the rug before her, looking at it critically.

'Do you? I'm not sure about it. I don't think hats with big brims do much for me. I've got a small face.'

'You've got small everything,' said Laurence. 'Small hands, small feet, small ankles, small wrists. You *are* small.' He turned and looked at her again. 'Aren't you?' He smiled.

Obviously he liked small people then. Well, he seemed to like her. The fragment of a silly popular song floated into her mind.

*I like LITTLE people –*
*Little, teeny-weeny, TINY little people –*
*Someone you can get hold of and throw across the road –*

She always thought of this as her song, and smiled to herself.

'Shall we go for a walk round the lake?' Laurence asked. He was staring ahead again.

Then he turned and offered her his hand. 'Come on – up you get.'

Muriel curled her legs round under her, tucking her feet under the hem of her dress.

'No. I want to stay here and think. You go.'

Laurence used his hands to get up off the rug in one movement. He was quite athletic. He had won medals for gymnastics. Which was odd. Odd because gymnasts should be good movers, yet Laurence didn't like dancing.

He looked down on her. 'Sure?' he asked.

'I don't want to walk. I want to think.'

'Shouldn't do too much thinking,' he said. 'It wrinkles the forehead. And you've got a nice forehead.'

A nice forehead! '*. . . I have a left shoulder that is a miracle* *of loveliness ... and my right elbow has a fascination few can resist ...'* the ugly Kati-Sha in *The Mikado*, which they had seen last week. Muriel had laughed till her ribs ached.

She smiled. 'Yes, and my right elbow—'

'Has a fascination that few can resist,' said Laurence.

He was smiling down at her and feeling in his jacket pocket for his cigarette case. Silver-plated, with 'ALM' engraved on it. Arthur Laurence Miles. No one ever called him Arthur, which was a good thing. They called him 'Loll' sometimes and he didn't seem to mind.

Taking one of his Players' Navy Cut out, he snapped the case shut and tapped the end of the cigarette on its flat surface. To shake off the loose shreds of tobacco. He always did that. He found his lighter in another pocket, flicked its little flame, put the cigarette in his mouth, lit it and inhaled deeply.

'Very well, then,' he said to her. 'I shall take a brief perambulation.'

Case and lighter were dropped back into his pocket, and he walked away towards the lake, blowing out a cloud of smoke. He paused with his back to her, looking at the view, his spare hand still in his trouser-pocket, clenching his buttocks in and out. Then he moved off, walking slowly, puffing contentedly.

Serious thinking, now. Muriel used the trunk of the oak tree they were sitting under to hold her back straight. It was knobbly and uncomfortable so it should keep her concentrating.

Should she marry him? Or should she not? She had the list of reasons for and against in her head. She closed her eyes.

Reasons to Marry Laurence Miles:

He is devoted, he is loyal, he is Always There.

He is funny.

He is clever.

He says he has loved me since he saw me sitting on the
　　pavement talking to the butcher's dog. (I don't
　　remember this. I'm sure I didn't do it.)

He has just passed his surveyor's exams.

He is the right height – not too tall.

He dresses well.

His mother is lovely.

That was a good start. Muriel opened her eyes and looked
across towards the lake.

You could see a long way, but the air was hot and soggy.
Her cotton frock was beginning to stick to her and she hated
this. Sweat gives you BO.

There were cries and a rhythmic *ping, pong, tong, thud*
coming from the tennis courts the other side of the trees – and
the noise of children playing 'He' somewhere behind her.
And a faint, rumbling growl.

Looking up at the sky she saw the anvil-shaped cloud – flat-
topped, the colour of sheet metal, rising above the tree-tops.
A thunderstorm. Of course. There would have to be a thunderstorm to spoil their day. *And* she was sitting under a tree.
It was a dangerous thing to do in a thunderstorm – although
she had forgotten why.

Norah said that thunder was caused by clouds bumping
together. It couldn't be true, though. Could it?

She closed her eyes again.

Reasons NOT to Marry Laurence Miles:

He is very quiet.

He doesn't like dancing.

He is sometimes touchy.

He doesn't make me feel happy and silly like Lidell used
   to.

He is not sociable.

He lives in a world of his own.

His sister is dreadful.

That was seven reasons against and *eight* reasons for. And she
was now nearly twenty-three years old, and no longer a
teenager. No longer the office mascot. The one they all loved
to laugh at. She was Sir Arthur's Personal Private Secretary
with Responsibilities. Her career as Office Entertainer was
over. And there was a new girl in the downstairs office now.
Blonde, blue-eyed and silly.

It was time to think of her future. No question.

Frank was married, Fred was married, even Kathleen was
married, though what sort of a life her husband was getting was
open to question – only Norah and Mollie were left at home.

The grumble rolled over the trees again – *Ping, pong,
boing* ... 'OOUUT!' went the tennis players. 'Got you!' called
the children. 'No! It's NOT FAIR!'

Muriel opened her eyes and pulled the basket towards her.
Inside it, apart from the pork pie and the sandwiches they
hadn't been able to eat, was a bottle of home-made lemonade.
And some picnic cups.

Finding the bottle, she unscrewed the top and poured some
into one of the cups.

As she screwed the bottle top back and balanced the cup in the grass, she thought how nice it was of Laurence's mother to say, 'Call me Mother Miles.' She needed a mother. She didn't have one any more. Of course, Laurence's mother was not like *her* mother – she was a bit overwhelming sometimes. Liked to take charge. But oh, what a cook she was! And how much she had taught her about cooking – roasts, casseroles (so much better than stews), 'pink fish' (salmon).

She took a sip of the lemonade. It was rather warm. But it was lovely.

The sun went in. The anvil-shaped cloud had turned into a Gothic castle, towering above – turreted, pinnacled and ominous. And Laurence had returned, standing over her, looking down and smiling.

'If we get married,' she said to him, 'will we book St Gabriel's Church?'

The first drop of rain splashed onto her face.

## Wedding Plans (1927)

'Well obviously Fred will have to give her away.'
'What about Frank?'
'He lives in Nottingham.'
'Yes, but he could get here.'
'He'd have to bring Ruby.'

'Oh my God. Yes. Of course.'

'And Fred will have to bring Greta . . .'

'And Dick's got to bring Lily. But that's all right. Lily's lovely.'

'I know; but I'm still thinking about Ruby and Greta.'

'It can't be helped. It's family. That's what family weddings are like.'

'Who's going to pay for all this? And what do we put on the invitations? *Mollie and Norah request the pleasure of your company on the occasion of the marriage of their sister, Muriel, to Arthur Laurence Miles . . .*?'

'I think Laurence's mother and father are going to help with the costs.'

'So should we put, *Mr and Mrs Charles Miles request the pleasure of your company on the occasion of the marriage of Mollie and Norah's sister, Muriel, to their son, Arthur Laurence . . .*?'

'That doesn't sound right.'

'No. It doesn't.'

'What do you think of him?'

'Who?'

'Laurence, of course. Dear old Loll.'

'Well, he's not a lot of fun. But he's all right. I mean – he sees the joke, doesn't he?'

'Mmm. I think there's more to Loll than meets the eye.'

'He's a bit serious.'

'You need a husband serious. All that silly nonsense with Lidell Savill. Waste of time. He was a playboy. Stood out a mile. And as for *Tom*.'

'Oh, he was nice, Tom was.'

'Yes, but RC, dear. It would have broken Mother's heart.'

'Her heart was broken already.'

'Mmm.'

'He's quite musical, I hear. Laurence is. And he's going to have a good job. Surveyor. Better paid than bank clerk.'

'Father was *chief* clerk.'

'Yes, but there was no money in it.'

'No. You need a husband serious and high earning. Well. Reasonably so.'

'She could do worse.'

'She could.'

'Your turn next, Norah!'

'Oh no. Not me. You can't trust men. Keep them on a string, dear. Keep them on a string.'


# Mrs Arthur Laurence Miles (1927)


She did not enjoy the wedding as much as she had hoped she would. The dressmaker made her dress a short one instead of down to the floor. Why hadn't the woman realised that the fashion had changed and short wedding dresses were OUT? It wasn't as if she had not specified precisely what she wanted. And it had cost enough. Maybe she should have made a stand and refused it when it was delivered. Except that it had been delivered one day before the wedding so there wouldn't have been time for alterations.

She looked out of the window of their small new sitting room into the plot which would eventually be the garden. Why was she miserable? A new house bought on a small mortgage, new furniture, a new husband, a new life. It was lovely, surely?

As for the bouquet. She had ordered a small bouquet – something else which was now fashionable – and been sent one as big as she was. She had been obliterated by it. Big bouquets were OUT for brides in 1927. They were fusty and old-fashioned. The short dress, the huge bunch of flowers – she looked dreadful in the wedding photos, she knew she did. Laurence looked handsome though, and there was no doubt he was the right height. Not too tall, not too short, but just right.

The problem was, she wondered if he *was* right after all.

There was a heavy step on the front path. Bother. The milkman would be at the door in a second and he would want paying.

Muriel got up from the arm of the chair on which she had settled during her dusting routine, left the duster on the coffee table and went into the kitchen for her purse. All bright and shiny the kitchen was – so different from Shoreditch, so different from Aberdeen Road. She lived in a delightful, modern, three-bedroom semi in a desirable residential area. What more could she want?

Walking into the narrow hall as she heard the knocker, she opened the front door, with its stained-glass rising sun motif above the letter-box. All the houses had them. The milkman's shining face appeared, grinning and nodding, his rough red hands outstretched with two bottles of milk dangling from them.

She took these and put them on the floor beside her.

'I expect you'd like your money,' she said to him, opening her purse.

'Yes, Mrs Miles. Ta,' he replied, the grin still fixed in position.

Being called 'Mrs Miles' still gave her a shock. She hoped she didn't look surprised, and counted out the coins carefully (wouldn't do to overpay him – he probably wouldn't tell her if she did and money was tight), putting them into his roughened palm.

He touched his milkman's cap, stretched the grin further, gathered up his hand-held crate of milk.

'Ta. Thanks. G' morning.' He swung down the path, through the front gate, clicking it behind him.

Back to the dusting, then. It had to be done. Every day. And the kitchen and bathroom floors mopped. And the supper cooked for Laurence. Using the new gas stove.

She dusted mechanically – start on the right and go round the room until you come to where you began. She picked up the wedding photo from the window-ledge, rubbing round the frame. There they were. Standing outside St Gabriel's Church.

Yes. That bouquet, that dress, that veil – it was all too much for her. You could just see her nose above the flowers and under the headdress. Where was Muriel on her wedding day? Where indeed?

She sighed and replaced the photograph.

The wedding had not been good. For one thing Mother had not been there. She had worn herself out, her beloved mother. She had just not bothered to come round from that anaesthetic. That was how Muriel saw it. Mother was exhausted – lost a daughter, lost a husband and died from the hardness of it all. No question.

Muriel dusted the window-ledge, still thinking.

Your little bit of life is what matters. She had seen a lot of death for a 24-year-old and that was her conclusion. You cling to life, whatever. It is always better than the alternative.

She opened one of the windows and shook the duster out of it. A cat surveyed her from the grass patch which was the front garden. A tabby. Like her beloved cat in Aberdeen Road.

'Hello,' she said quietly. 'Come and talk to me.'

The cat looked at her steadily, then turned and walked away to complete whatever errand he was on.

She closed the window, and moved to the mantelpiece.

That was another thing. Taggy was dead. He had become very old and she had stopped loving him. She had grown out of him and grown into young men. That was normal, wasn't it?

But she had abandoned him. Her faithful friend. That wasn't right.

Oh, good heavens, he was only a cat! True. But cats have feelings. They need loving.

She dusted under the clock, before turning her attention to the mirror above.

Then there had been the honeymoon disaster.

Poor Laurence. It hadn't been his fault the 'hotel' had only been a village pub – he hadn't realised it. But he should have known. He was a man. Men were supposed to look after things like that. The bedroom was dirty and smelt of beer and you could hear the noise from the public bar until all hours. The shame and misery of it all meant he had been unable to do what a man was supposed to do on his wedding night. In the morning they had moved out to a proper hotel for the rest of the time and he had got better. But she didn't like it. If it weren't for the fact that she wanted children, she probably would never let him do it again. But then, men expect it, it seemed. He would have to be rationed.

Finishing the mirror she started on the coffee table. What was it Laurence had told her about a cartoon in *Punch*? Oh, yes, a man was tripping over a small table like this one and saying, 'The trouble with these occasional tables is they are too frequent.' That had made her laugh. Laurence had a good sense of humour, but he was so touchy, so sensitive and moody. Came of being too clever by half. Better never to think that deeply. She made sure she didn't. Does you no good. No question.

Moving over to the bookshelf, she carefully shifted the books and dusted behind them.

In the evening after he had eaten supper, all Laurence wanted to do was read his book. Why? She enjoyed reading, too, but she preferred talking, any day. Why couldn't he talk to her? She spent boring hours, days and weeks at home seeing only the milkman and she wanted a conversation. She asked him why he wouldn't talk to her and he said, 'I haven't got anything to say.'

Mother had said that to her when she had first brought him home. 'Isn't he rather a *quiet* young man for you, dear?'

He *was* quiet. But he was reliable. Laurence had always been there for her, standing waiting, holding an umbrella if it was raining. That was good. And loving Lidell had been bad. Waste of time even thinking about him.

She shook the duster out of the window again. The cat was nowhere to be seen. Perhaps she and Laurence could get a kitten?

She closed the window. A kitten would be fun – but it would cost money to keep and feed.

Thank God for sisters. Mollie and Norah. She could call them at any time and chat for hours on end – only she didn't, because of the telephone bills.

She looked round the room. Spotless. How she had to have it. The cushions needed plumping though. Then she would think about supper.

A shepherd's pie, perhaps?

# The Operation (1931)

It was such a blow. A real blow, as well as a shock to the system.

It had been a glorious day for watching a tennis match. Too hot, if the truth were told, but Muriel had been wearing a white, short-sleeved dress and a floppy sun hat, and had felt comfortable – especially since she and Laurence were sitting on chairs arranged underneath the chestnut tree.

And there they had been. At the tennis club, watching the

mixed doubles final. Laurence in an open-necked shirt and grey flannels with his hair un-Brylcreemed, looking handsome and casual with his fawn mac on his lap (he never went anywhere without it), puffing on a Navy Cut cigarette, and she with her feet in their high-heeled shoes tucked neatly beneath her and her straw clutch handbag on her lap. Watching the white figures dashing to and fro, listening to the clatter of china from the pavilion as the helpers got the tea ready.

Lovely. She enjoyed a good tennis match, although she knew she was not a good player herself. All she had done was turn to Laurence and say, 'I think Brian and Audrey are going to win this,' when it happened. Bang. Right into the side of her neck. The tennis ball. At high speed.

She thought for a second she was dead. Laurence put an arm round her, people got up from their chairs and came round to see if she was all right, and play on the court was suspended.

Holding her hand to her neck and trying not to cry with the pain and surprise of it, she had said of course she was all right, it was only a tennis ball, good heavens, nothing serious, please don't worry. All those things. And then they had gone in for tea and play had resumed afterwards. Brian and Audrey won and she and Laurence had gone home.

But the next morning she noticed a small lump on her neck.

And the next morning it was bigger.

'Well, go and see Dr Barker, if it worries you that much,' Laurence had said, as she was standing in front of the mirror, prodding the lump and peering at it.

Dr Barker knew everything. Of course, Laurence was

right. Dr Barker would answer her questions and put her mind at rest.

What was the peculiar lump on her neck? It was a straightforward question.

And the straightforward answer was – not straightforward.

'You've suffered a blow to the thyroid gland,' Dr Barker had said.

'What does that mean?' she had asked.

'Well, you've grown what we call a goitre. A small goitre. Not serious, Muriel.'

'What do we do about it?'

'We do nothing about it,' he had said cheerily. 'Let me show you out.'

A goitre. She looked it up in the dictionary. *A morbid, often enormous, enlargement of the thyroid gland in the neck.*

She thought of what she had heard about goitres. And thought and thought. Until her nights were haunted by huge growths; enormous, purple, bigger than the necks that carried them. She had visions of people, dragging themselves around with hideous excrescences on their throats.

A goitre. It could affect her children if she became pregnant. Her children would be born deformed, sickly, unable to thrive. Oh God. A GOITRE! She had known a man with a goitre in his neck. Bigger than a football. She would be like that. Weighed down. Unable to conceive anything but blighted children. She wanted children. What would happen to the boy and the girl she wished for? What was the point of enduring what you had to endure between the sheets if her wish for a baby were destroyed? What if? What if? What if?

After two weeks of this her husband spoke. 'Mrs H'em,' he had said, adopting the jocular, Dickensian tone he used sometimes to make her laugh. 'Mrs H'em – it seems to me you are getting in a two-and-eight about this matter. You are coming over all unnecessary. Go to Dr Barker again for heaven's sake and stop making our lives a misery.'

So Mrs Muriel Miles trotted down to the doctor's again, sleepless and agitated.

'What will happen to my children? What will happen to me? I shall be disfigured . . .'

'Muriel, Muriel, you must stop letting your imagination run away with you,' Dr Barker had said, twiddling with his pen over his blotter.

He had looked up at her.

'I can see what this is doing to you emotionally. I assure you it will do you no harm physically, but because of the former consideration I am going to recommend you have an operation to remove the lump.'

And now she was in this lovely hospital with kind nurses in white starched headdresses making a fuss of her.

They gave her a mirror to look at the small scar with the stitches on her throat. They promised her it would never show. And the dreadful lump was gone.

She leant back on her pillows and took a grape from the bowl in front of her on the table across her bed.

She looked at the calm, ordered scene before her as the nurses went about their business, pulling curtains round beds, taking patients out of the ward in wheelchairs, sitting by bedsides, taking temperatures. Everything neat, tidy, comfortable and as it should be. The reassuring disinfectanty smell was all around her, mixed with the faint aroma of a rather nice supper cooking. She felt safe.

And here was Laurence walking across the ward with an enormous bunch of carnations. She only wished she liked carnations. But it was the thought that counted.

# The Unwanted Pregnancy (1935)

As a young girl she'd been pretty. Fairly pretty. Oval face, pale as an egg; half-smiling mouth – or was it wincing? – a good deal of wild hair, and large eyes, sloping down at the corners. 'Newmarch eyes'. Sitting for the photographer in a floppy, knitted sailor hat (her 'tobby hat' she'd called it) and her best sailor blouse with the square collar and the handsome bow. An E. Nesbitt child. Fourteen or fifteen. Just at the end of the First World War. When they had lived over the bank, in Shoreditch High Street, next to a jellied eel stall.

Why this photograph had been at the bottom of the box of pictures of John when he was born, she had no idea. It should have been in the bath-salts box with the ones of her mother and her brothers and sisters all that time ago. She put it on her lap and closed her eyes for a minute.

Seventeen years. It had to be seventeen years. She was thirty-two now. And worried out of her life. Her eyes shot open.

It should not have happened. She never intended it to happen. Not now. Not at this moment. John was only two. Why did she have to be pregnant again? Where was the money coming from? It didn't grow on trees. Not in their house.

She looked round. A modest, new-build, three-bedroomed suburban semi, in New Southgate. Cost them £300 and they had a mortgage. Settee, two matching chairs, dining table, four chairs. Upstairs a child's cot, another chair and a large, uncomfortable double bed.

It wasn't as if she enjoyed it. The stuff in the marital bed. Never had. She had no idea why anybody did, if anybody did. Women, that is. She wouldn't know, as obviously it's not something you talk about.

Maybe she wasn't pregnant. But Alice should have come last week. And hadn't.

'Alice, where art thou?' – that's what Mollie used to sing if she was Late. All the girls in the family did it too. But as none of them was married then, being Late was never a worry.

Not like today.

She put the box of photographs back in the drawer, and sat in the armchair again (wooden arms, velvet cushions and a movable back – very modern). She picked up the cup of tea balanced on the arm and took a sip. She didn't often get the chance to sit down, these days. John needed constant attention. But Mollie was looking after him this morning. Thank heavens for sisters! How many times had she said that?

Never go on holiday. John had been conceived on holiday. It's holidays that do it. No question.

She knew there had been a mistake. She had run to the hotel bathroom and douched immediately afterwards. She always did, anyway. You don't want to take chances. Seemed it had done no good.

Nor had jumping down the last four stairs, over and over again.

A very hot bath, then, and a glass of gin and orange.

Lying back in the steam later, with the glass at her elbow on the cork-topped stool, she imagined how the heat and the alcohol would work to loosen the hold of this incubus. If she wished it hard enough, surely it would all come away? It was only tiny.

She looked at her breasts, floating in the water, their nipples chestnut brown, the blue veins standing out. But then, they had looked like that since John. Things happen to bodies when you have babies. Things she didn't like much. But she didn't like bodies anyway. Especially hers.

Her legs were short and definitely bandy. Her hips were broad. Her hands and feet were tiny (that was good, though – she liked her hands and feet) and she was under five feet tall. Probably an inch under.

She sighed and pulled the plug out, watching the scummy water swirling past her and down the drain. Not a scrap of blood or guts in it anywhere.

Perhaps this one would be a girl. She'd wanted a girl. Though not just now.

# The Toad (1936)

The only good thing to be said about this pregnancy was that it was going to end in May – before the hot weather started.

It was April now. Muriel felt large and clumsy as she walked to the shops with three-year-old John on his reins.

She also felt tired as this baby was lively and kept her awake at night kicking her with its tiny feet. Laurence kept her awake anyway, snoring, so she was getting used to life without sleep. She supposed that married women always felt tired. It was one of those things you Just Put Up With – like all the rest of it.

The pavements were wet from the last shower. Wet and gleaming. John now decided it was fun to squat down and put his hands on them to see what made them shine. She bent over and pulled him upright.

'Look at those muddy hands,' she said as she studied them. 'I'll have to dab you.'

Still holding his reins, she managed to undo her bag and extract her hankie. She rubbed it over his grubby hands, held them palm up, for inspection, turned them over, looked at the backs and decided they would pass muster. She stuffed the handkerchief back into her bag and clicked it shut, and she and John carried on their slow progress along the road.

The cherry trees were in full blossom, petals falling in confetti showers onto the neat squares of wet earth in which they stood at regular intervals along the kerbside. April. Everything burgeoning and blooming.

'Won't it be nice,' she said to John as they walked, 'won't it be nice to have a new little brother or sister, John?'

Her little boy stopped in his tracks and turned round to her. He looked surprised, as if he had been interrupted in some private train of thought.

'What, Mummy?' he asked.

She bent down to him, as far as she could manage. 'A new little brother or sister, darling. Next month. Are you looking forward to it?'

He fixed round eyes on her face as he considered this.

'Could we have a lorry instead?' he asked.

She stood up, laughing.

'I don't think I could manage a lorry, John,' she said.

The child was so like his father. Eccentric, self-absorbed. Too clever by half. She worried about him sometimes – he was so un-childlike.

He had already sensibly lost interest in the possibility of a lorry, and was wandering along ahead of her, tugging at the reins.

Muriel took a half-step forward – and froze. Her left leg was extended, her neat Cuban-heeled shoe next to the base of one of the cherry trees. (Dr Barker had told her she shouldn't wear her high heels during pregnancy, but she had taken no notice of him.) It wasn't the heeled shoe that was the problem. It was what was about to crawl onto it.

From the muddy square of earth in which the tree was planted emerged a green creature – maybe more mud-coloured than green, mottled would be a better description – webbed feet planted before it, its skin gleaming with moisture and a long comb extending down its back. Huge eyes and a bulging throat confronted her. Then, horror of horrors, its left front leg moved forward as if to meet hers – indeed, as if to climb up the inside of her leg.

She let out a little shriek of fright. John turned round to see what was happening. He moved towards her and squatted down to look at the nightmare in front of her.

'Toad, Mummy,' he said. 'Only old toad.'

But to Muriel there was no such thing as only an old toad. Or only an old frog, for that matter. She had a loathing of both which she had to admit had been passed on to her from her mother.

What would this do to the baby?

She was transfixed with terror, her leg extended, the toad's leg extended, all sorts of fears fighting in her head. Possibly the toad had fears fighting in its head also, but that was not her concern.

John got up, and tugged her hand.

'Only old toad, Mummy. Come on.'

The spell was broken and she moved away from the tree as the toad continued its crawl towards the privet hedge of Number 31.

That should have been the end of the incident, but Muriel had learnt how to worry early in life and this encounter had upset her. She kept thinking about it. A toad. Toads were associated with witches, with curses, with all manner of evil. A sudden meeting like that while she was pregnant could affect the unborn child. Bound to. No question. Her baby was cursed. What a catastrophe! Who could she talk to? Not Laurence – he already thought she was an Anxious Mother.

So a week later Muriel *tap, tapped* her way slowly down the hill to see Dr Barker.

Dr Barker put his hands together and his elbows on his desk that bright morning – sunbeams on his blotter. Then he leant his head on his hands and looked at her the way he had done all those years ago when she had visited him about her legs.

'It's bound to affect the baby, a shock like that, isn't it?' she said. 'That's what I worry about.'

'Oh dear,' said Dr Barker. 'Where have you got such a silly old wives' tale from? It's all nonsense. The baby is fine, *you* are fine, everything is as it should be, and next month you are going to give birth to a perfectly normal baby. Seeing a toad can't make any difference. You know that really.'

She was reassured – somewhat. All the same, old wives' tales often have some truth in them.

'And why are you still wearing those unsuitable shoes?' asked Dr Barker as she got up to leave.

'Because I can't walk in flats,' she answered, making her escape.

She wasn't going to fuss about shoes. But toads. Toads were a different matter.

# The New Baby (1936)

Muriel and Judith Mary stared at each other.

She had entered the world easily, with no stress and not

much pain. Muriel had almost enjoyed the experience and was lying back on her bed in her own bedroom holding the scarlet rag of humanity in her arms, studying her in detail.

It was five o'clock in the afternoon on a cold May day. Fires were lit all over the house and she even had the bedside lamps on. The midwife was downstairs making a cup of tea, and bed, baby and mother were tidied up and spotless. But Judith Mary appeared not to like being spotless and was wriggling and squawling.

Odd. When John was born he lay in her arms sleepily, his eyes closed and his long lashes resting on his cheeks. This one appeared to have eyes everywhere and was threshing about trying to get up and start doing things.

Muriel had already unwrapped and upended her to make sure she was present and correct with no fearsome deformities or noticeable defects. The only imperfection she could see was a small birthmark on the inside of Judith's left calf. In the shape of a toad. Well, it looked like a toad. When Judith was older she would tell her about that.

A girl. Just what she had ordered. And talkative, judging from the noise she was making. The baby squinted at her, waving her small arms and grimacing. Was she smiling at Mummy? No. Newborn babies don't smile. And yet – was she pleased to see her? To see Mummy? This mummy, who would protect her like a lioness, a mummy who would put her first come what may, who would love her unconditionally whatever she did?

Judith arched her back and glared round the room, looking for an escape route. She obviously didn't think much of being hampered by infancy, trammelled by shawls, nappies, midwives and mummies.

Muriel would lie down and die for her. She knew she would. If she had to.

A daughter. Maybe she would be able to talk to her? Have conversations? John was three but he didn't talk to her; Laurence never talked to her – maybe here was someone who would listen to her? Someone she could tell her story to: Shoreditch, Lucy, Father, Mother, working at Savill's, and of course the ancestral tale of the Newmarch family going right back to William the Conqueror. Although there were a few gaps in that. Never mind, they could be filled in.

A 'bonded child'. All the baby books said that was what was wanted. For the psychological and physical health of the child. Judith would be bonded. Judith would be her confidante, Judith would be the person with whom she would hold a conversation which would last for the whole of their lives. Judith would have a mummy who would *always* have time to talk to her.

A daughter! You can say *anything* you like to your own daughter. No question.

Outside, a chilly evening descended. The three-bedroomed semi contemplated the others opposite, sitting quietly by the side of the road, a mirror image of its neighbours, except for the smoke that was billowing out of the chimney. And Arthur Laurence Miles was making his way quickly up the hill towards it, to greet his new infant, briefcase in hand, rolled umbrella over arm, trilby on head.

Inside, Sister Flo was taking a tray of tea upstairs to Mrs Miles, and Judith Mary Miles was screaming her head off.

# JUDITH'S STORY

# The Walk With Father (1939)

I went out with Daddy this morning. I was in my pushchair although I can walk. Something went wrong with one of the wheels and Daddy said a word. 'DAMNATIONTAKEIT.' I thought it was a good word. I'll use it if ever I have to mend a pushchair.

Now I'm in the garden. I have walked down the path in the sun and I'm wearing socks and sandals. I have a dress on with a full skirt and flowers on it. And puffed sleeves. I feel nice in it.

Here's a patch of pink flowers with pale green leaves all round. The leaves aren't like the leaves of other plants. They are fat like green flippers. She says this is sweetallison. I bend down and put my hands on my knees so that I can see it better. I put one hand out and feel the leaves. They're cold and thick. I put my hand back on my knee and look at the flowers. There are furry insects all over them making a noise. They come and go and settle and buzz and go again. They are buzzy and busy. They're bees. She said they are bees. The plant looks as if it is alive and breathing in and out with the bees.

I'll stay like this, looking at the flowers and the bees, in my cotton dress and my socks and sandals and my hands on my knees. I'll stay like this for a long time because I make a picture. If anyone looks over the fence and they see me, they'll think, what a pretty picture. That little girl in her flowery dress looking at the flowers.

But she is coming to take me in for something to eat. She talks to me. And she laughs. Even if she's cross with me I can see she is laughing. I make her laugh often. She says I would laugh to see a pudding crawl. Mummy.

I take her hand and go into the house, up the back steps. The paint on the door is hot and has bubbles on it. I'd like to burst them, but we have to go into the dining room. I'll burst them later.

I sit at the table. It has a white cloth on it. But I don't want to eat. If I'm hungry I go outside and eat the bits of bread on the lawn. She throws it there every evening. She is cross when I eat it. And then she laughs at me.

She gives me some stewed apple.

'Do you want cream on it, Judith?'

No, I don't.

'Your last chance. There won't be any cream next weekend.'

'Why not?'

'Because there is a war on.'

What is a war?

At bedtime I ask her, what is a war? She says it's when people fight each other and drop bombs. Will they drop bombs on us I want to know. She says Daddy is digging us an airaidshelter in the garden and we will be safe in there. She says I need not worry as we will always be safe in our house or in our shelter.

She looks at me and puts her finger on my nose, wobbling

it backwards and forwards. She says, 'Goodnight, Bunny-nose. Come Mummy.'

She opens her arms. 'Come Mummy. Give Mummy a kiss.'

So I do.

She goes, but she leaves the light on. I have to have the light on. I'd like her to come back now. I would like her to stay with me.

'Mummy,' I call. 'Can I have a glass of water?'

'There she goes. And I've only just put her to bed,' I hear her say.

# The Drum (1941)

I am in bed because I have been naughty. I didn't mean to be naughty. I just wanted something to happen. I like it when things happen. I threw an egg at the dining-room curtains last week. That was because I wanted something to happen.

The milkman delivered the eggs and the milk and I just grabbed one out of the box and ran with it. I don't know why I did that, but it seemed a good idea at the time.

Then my brother chased me. Which made it exciting. And I could hear him shouting, 'Judith! Don't!' I thought, 'John thinks I am going to throw this egg, so I will.' I hadn't thought of it before. And having him running after me, all hot and anxious, made it feel like the clowns at the circus.

I got into our dining room, and the curtains were still drawn. The sun was trying to get through the cracks, though, because it was morning. I held the egg in my hand and John was just catching up with me, and Mummy was at the door still with the milkman shouting, 'Stop her, John!' and I thought this will be a happening. A proper happening. So I lifted up the egg and bent back my arm and I threw it at the curtains. It broke and a lot of slimy yellow stuff slipped down the brown velvet. It looked like a painting. I enjoyed doing it very much.

But Mummy was cross with me and John looked sorry and as if it was his fault. He is nice to me, my brother. I hit him with the poker once and he was still nice. Of course, I didn't mean to hit him with the poker. It was an accident. Sort of.

Throwing the egg was naughty, though. They told me it was. But it wasn't as naughty as I've been today – which is why I am in bed and it's still daylight outside.

It's my brother's birthday – he is eight today. Three years older than me. But he is upset. And I did it. Upset him.

I did it this morning when he unwrapped all his presents. He had a lot of nice things – some books and a cowboy outfit and a toy gun – and this round parcelly thing. I couldn't think what it could be and neither could he.

'Open it! Open it, John!' I cried. I was jumping up and down with excitement.

'This will be a real surprise,' said Mummy, as she watched him pulling the paper off. Daddy was watching too, with a sort of pleased smile.

'Get him the scissors,' said Mummy to Daddy, as John was fighting with the string stuff.

It was such a moment. Mummy and me and John all sitting

on the floor with this round parcel, and Daddy going out of the room for the scissors.

I could see a bird on the concrete outside our dining-room windows. A big black bird, pecking at the crumbs from last night's supper. We have windows in doors that open so you can see low down to the ground. I lay on my stomach watching the bird, while Daddy fetched the scissors.

Daddy helped John get the string and the paper off, and when it was all in a bundle we could see what it had been wrapped round.

It was a drum — with drumsticks. A proper drum. Not a tin drum, but one with sort of skin across it.

'Daddy went all the way to the Houndsditch Warehouse for that,' said Mummy. 'It's a real drum — amazing — we didn't think we would be able to get one in wartime.'

John was so pleased. He looped the belt over his shoulder and walked about batting the drum with the drumsticks. Daddy put his fingers in his ears.

'We may regret this purchase,' he said to Mummy.

Mummy picked up all the untidy bits of wrapping and string and went into the kitchen.

John marched round and round like a soldier with his drum, and Daddy went outside. He doesn't like noise.

John was so pleased he didn't even say thank you. Just went round and round batting.

'Come and have some lunch,' said Mummy from the kitchen. 'We're having it early so that we can get ready for the party later.'

We all sat round the kitchen table to eat, but it was marrow in cheese sauce and it was horrible.

'Well, you wouldn't wait with me in the fish queue yesterday,' said Mummy. 'I told you I only had a marrow and some cheese at home and you said, "Oh that will be all right – anything just so long as we don't have to wait in this queue." You know you said that. No question.'

John tried to eat his, because it was true what Mummy said. But it had been a long fish queue, in Middleton Road, and it had been raining. We didn't want to wait and we had both tugged at Mummy's hand and pulled her away.

Daddy pushed his around the plate and then left his knife and fork neatly in the middle and went into the sitting room for a cigarette.

And I said, 'Please may I get down?' although I was already half off my stool anyway, and Mummy said, 'Aren't you going to eat this? There's nothing else! There's a war on!' as I left.

I went to look at John's presents in the dining room. And I particularly wanted to see the drum.

It was in the middle of the floor – shiny and new. It had red and blue stripes painted on it and a rope with tassels round it. It looked smart. I found the drumsticks lying by it and did a *rat-tat-tat* on it with them. Then I put them down and stroked the top of the drum. It was smooth and cool. It was skin, Mummy had said. But it was quite thin skin. Thin like an eggshell.

Suddenly I had a vision of a happening. A good happening. Something that would bring everybody running to see it. I knew how it would be if I did it. So I did it.

I jumped into the drum. There was a thump and the thin skin tore. I was standing right inside it. What a happening it was.

Just for a moment I felt good. But when Mummy and John came running in from the kitchen, John burst into tears. And I didn't like seeing him cry. But it was too late then.

And Mummy was cross. I have never seen her so cross. She sat me down in a corner and said I would not be coming to the party.

Daddy came in and said, 'What the blazes has she done now?' He hates things to get horrible. And they had got horrible.

John cried and cried, holding his ruined drum, and Mummy talked to me and talked to me. She said how long she and Daddy had searched for the drum, and what it had cost and how much John had wanted one. Then she said, 'You are destructive, Judith. That's what you are. Destructive.'

She got up and walked away, as if she hated me. And John wouldn't look at me.

But I thought 'destructive' was a good word. I kept thinking about it, and saying it to myself. 'Destructive.' I wondered how many people were destructive or if I was the only one. I hugged the word to myself. My secret self. Destructive.

They got the party ready and nobody spoke to me. Nobody looked at me. That was odd, because I thought being destructive had made me special. And it had. But in the wrong way. I had lost everybody. Nobody thought well of me. It wasn't a good feeling.

I watched the sandwiches and the biscuits being carried through to our front room where tea was being laid on a white cloth. And Mummy had made jellies with hundreds and thousands on. I watched those going in too. And she didn't smile at me once.

Then she said, 'You are going to bed now, Judith,' and she took me by the hand, made me go into the bathroom and rubbed a flannel over my face. Then she led me into my bedroom and took off my clothes and put my pyjamas on.

'Into bed,' she said. Just like that.

I got into bed and pulled the bedclothes up to my chin, looking at her.

She didn't look back, and went across the room to draw my blue curtains, although it wasn't dark. As she went out of the room she said, 'Now stay there and think about what you have done.'

And I have thought and thought and decided that although it was a good happening it wasn't a good thing to do. And now I want everything to be as it was before I did it. When Mummy and Daddy and John loved me.

The noise of the party downstairs has faded now, and I think I have heard our front door shut a lot of times. This may mean everyone has gone home. All John's friends, with their mummies.

Has anybody remembered me, I wonder. I'm hungry. I haven't had any tea and I didn't eat any marrow. Even though I am naughty, I should not be allowed to starve.

There are footsteps coming up the stairs. Quick, light footsteps. Mummy's footsteps. She is opening my bedroom door. Will she still be cross?

She stands by the bed, in her pretty party dress, and looks at me. I love this party dress she wears. It is dark blue with little golden elephants all over, and it swirls round her and floats out when she runs down the stairs in it.

I put my hand out and touch it. It feels silky.

'Well?' she says. 'Have you thought?'

She sits on the bed and takes my hand. She looks worried. I screw up my face at her and she laughs.

'Don't do that, Judith. I'm cross with you.'

I put my tongue out and touch my nose, making my eyes go funny.

'Judith,' she says, choking. 'I am not laughing at you.'

But she *is* laughing at me.

I lean forward and lick the back of her hand, like a kitten. Then I put my arms round her. 'Mummy, Mummy, I'm sorry I'm destructive,' I say. 'I didn't mean it. Please don't hate me. I didn't mean it.'

She cuddles me.

'There, there, darling,' she says. 'We know you didn't mean it. But you mustn't do things without thinking about them. It will get you into trouble.'

She kisses me. 'My bad Doodie,' she says.

It's all right. When she calls me 'Doodie' she loves me.

'I'm not a bad Doodie any more, Mummy,' I say.

'No,' she says. 'The bad Doodie has flown out of the house and is going away over the chimney-pots. There she goes. All gone! Shall I bring you a sandwich and a glass of milk?' she asks.

'Yes, please,' I say. 'Tell John I didn't mean it, Mummy.'

She feels in the pocket of her dress.

'He knows that, darling,' she says. 'He's given you a sweet from his sweet-ration tin.' She holds up her hand with a toffee in it.

'Don't eat it now. Eat it after your sandwich. And before you clean your teeth.'

She puts the toffee down on my bedside table, next to my Peter Rabbit book, and goes out, closing the door behind her.

When she's gone, I wonder was it true to say I didn't mean it? I *did* mean to jump in the drum. But I didn't mean to upset everyone. I didn't mean to make my brother cry. So I *didn't* mean it. I never will hurt anybody again – it makes you feel bad.

I listen. It is quiet, except for the sound of Daddy blowing his nose. John isn't crying. And now I can hear Mummy's quick steps on the stairs – coming to me with my sandwich and my milk. I think everything is going to be all right.

# The Night Before Christmas (1942)

It is very dark in our front room. That is because we have black things over our windows. Mummy calls it 'The Black Out'. You have to have it in case your lights show and The Enemy spot you and bomb you. There is a man who patrols the streets outside and he calls 'Put that light out!', so you know if your lights are showing.

But over there in the corner of the room, something is gleaming. I can see it glinting although it is dark. I've come into the front room so that I can see it, because I know it's here.

It's an exciting thing and tonight's an exciting night.

If I put the light on I'll be able to see this exciting thing properly, but I have to stand on tiptoe to reach the switch as it is high up on the wall.

It is quite cold in the front room. We have a fire alight in our dining room, where we sit in the evenings. Mummy and Daddy and my brother are all in there in the warm listening to the radio, but I have crept in here.

I must be careful, because in the middle of the room there is this big metal air-raid shelter and it hurts if you fall into it. It has sharp corners. Sometimes we use the top as a table and the cold metal edge of it presses on my bare legs while I sit at it. It is a Morrison shelter. For indoors. Outdoor ones are Anderson shelters, but ours filled up with water and frogs after a few months so we stopped using it.

We all sleep underneath this shelter. It's quite comfortable but a bit crowded.

I can hear the radio through the wall now – there are people laughing and I can hear my father and brother laughing too.

I wish I could reach the light switch.

*SNAP!* It's on. The light is on. The central light in the ceiling with the chains and the glass bowl with a spiderwebby pattern in it. It is shining in my eyes.

And Mummy is at the door, with her hand on the switch.

'Whatever are you doing in here, Judith?'

I look past her, to the glinting object in the corner. It's standing on top of a small cupboard. It is beautiful. It's a little tree with sparkling things hanging on it.

'Oh – the *Christmas tree*!' she says.

'Can I look at it, Mummy?'

'Of course you can look at it. But don't touch it. Some of the baubles are very old and they are made of glass, you know.'

I move closer to the magic tree. It has a square wooden base, painted white with garlands of holly and berries going round it. And on every branch there is a treasure. They are the baubles. Here is a round gold thing, like a coin but fatter – and here is another gold thing, hanging like a pendant. It is ridged all round.

'I said, don't touch, didn't I, darling? If you break one of those you will cut your hand.'

'Where did they come from, Mummy?'

'From my home. When I was a child we had this – it's amazing how it's all lasted.'

Clipped to each branch is a metal candle-holder with a candle in.

'Can we light the candles?'

'Maybe tomorrow. If Daddy is here to make sure it's safe.'

Mummy puts her hand out to me. 'Come on, it's your bed-time.'

Outside, the wailing starts. It's a funny wailing that makes you feel as if your stomach is falling out. Up and down. Up and down. The air-raid warning always starts at my bedtime. That's how we know it's my bedtime.

But tonight isn't any old bedtime. Looking round the room I can see the cardboard Santa and his reindeer that Mummy has fixed across the mantelpiece. And attached to the light and looping out to the corners of the ceiling are the paper chains my brother made last week.

'But it's Christmas!' I yell.

'Shh— Keep your voice down,' says Mummy.

The wailing noise starts to fade. It goes down and down and down, like an animal dying. I don't know which is worse, when it wails or when it dies.

'It's still bedtime,' she says. 'If you don't go to bed Father Christmas won't visit.' She laughs and wobbles my nose with her finger. 'But if you get into your pyjamas and dressing gown, Bunny-nose, I'll read something to you.'

'What?' I don't need reading to. I can read for myself.

'Something Christmassy and special, that we can enjoy together,' she says.

I go upstairs to the bathroom. It is really cold up here. I don't want to stay too long, but I wash my face and clean my teeth, go to my bedroom and put my pyjamas and my green woolly dressing-gown on. Then I go to the lavatory and run down the stairs after I've pulled the chain so that I get to the bottom before it stops flushing. If you don't do that the ghosts get you.

Outside the guns start banging. There are aircraft bumbling overhead. Theirs, I think. They sound different from ours. They sound sinister and threatening. Definitely theirs, then.

In the front room Mummy is sitting on one of the cushions on the floor by the Anderson with a paper-backed book in her hands. I crawl inside the shelter, and lie under the covers, listening to the explosions and the gunfire.

Then she starts reading.

*'Twas the night before Christmas,*
*And all through the house,*
*Not a creature was stirring —*

*Not even a mouse.*
*The stockings were hung by the chimney with care*
*In the hope that St Nicholas soon would be there . . .*

There is a loud bang, the room shakes, and she puts a cushion over my head and holds me for a few minutes.

'That was close,' she says, picking up the book again.


# The Illness (1943)


I am sitting with Mummy on our two-seater settee arrangement. It has wooden arms and an adjustable back, and you can tilt it back or forwards and fix it with a rod across the back that fits into slots. And it has brown velvet cushions with gold cord edgings. It's comfortable, particularly when I lean against Mummy.

Daddy is reading a book. He is always reading a book. When he finishes one, he picks up the next from the pile beside him and starts reading that.

Mummy has a cup of tea balanced on the flat wooden arm of our two-seater thing, and she is dipping a biscuit into it. She takes a bite and puts it back on the saucer.

My brother is playing the piano in the next room. I am just sprawling there. But I'm thinking.

Thinking how funny the clock on the mantelpiece looks.

First it is one clock, and then another clock slides out from behind it and it is two clocks. I move my head slightly and look at the candlestick at the end of the mantelpiece. It does the same. A ghostly second candlestick slides out, and it is two candlesticks.

'Mummy,' I say. 'I can see two clocks.'

'What, darling?' says Mummy, putting down her teacup.

'Two clocks,' I say. 'And two candlesticks. I can see two of everything.'

I look at Daddy in his chair. A shadowy second Daddy sits behind him. This is interesting.

'I am seeing double, Mummy,' I tell her.

Mummy looks across at Daddy.

'I think we ought to take her to get her eyes tested, dear, don't you?' she says, turning to her cup and saucer and picking them up with her left hand. She moves the arm she had round me to the handle of the cup and sips, looking across at him.

Daddy goes on reading.

'Don't you, dear?' she asks again, louder.

Daddy puts his book down on his lap.

'Did what, which, when, why?' he says.

'Judith's eyesight. It ought to be tested. She's seeing double.'

'Oh. Yes. Whatever you think.' He goes back to his book.

The double clocks are saying half-past eight, so it is my bedtime. Mummy finishes her tea and her biscuit and says, 'Come on; upsy-daisy.'

She takes my hand as I get off the settee. 'Up we go,' she says. 'Up the stairs.'

Together we go up to my bedroom, and I get into my dressing-gown while Mummy runs my bath.

I like having a bath. Mummy sits on the cork stool beside me and soaps my back and all my bits, and then I lie down in the water and put the flannel on my tummy. I pat it down and make sure it is really wet and sticking to me. Then I pull it up from the centre and it goes *SLURP, SQUELCH*, as it comes off. I lift up my leg and look at the funny mark on it. Like a toad. Mummy says it is a birthmark and that it is nothing. But I can see two of it. Mummy says, 'Out you get.'

I stand up in the bath and she wraps a big towel round me as I step out onto the bathmat. She rubs me all over and then takes my pyjamas out of the airing cupboard.

When I put them on they feel warm and clean.

'Bed now,' she says as she takes me into my bedroom and I climb in between the sheets.

She tucks me in and kisses me goodnight. 'Night, night, my Doodie,' she says. 'Tomorrow we'll take you to the optician.'

She goes, and leaves my door partly open so that I can see the light from the hall slanting in on the carpet. I look at it. I can see two strips of light.

And I can't sleep properly. Funny things start dancing in my head. Fat sponges, yellow and white, some big, some small. The big ones are frightening. I think they will suffocate me. They dance towards me and get huge. They are trying to get into my face. I feel sick. My head aches. I am hot. The sponges advance and retreat. I think of the Lobster Quadrille in *Alice*. I turn over. Wherever I put my head the sponges are there. Inside it. Smothering me. My limbs have turned into huge sponges as well. Enormous, thick, heavy and strange.

In the morning I cannot get up. Mummy takes my temperature and says, 'Good heavens!' She goes downstairs and I hear her talking to Daddy.

'I think she may have chickenpox – but she hasn't got a rash that I can see.'

I am ill. I don't care what it is, it is awful. My head is going round with the big sponges flying up and down in it, trying to get into my face; trying to get up my nose; trying to stifle me. I don't want to eat. If I think of food, I feel sick and the sponges come flying at me. I want Mummy. I want Mummy to read to me. Read to me, Mummy. Read to me.

'Once upon a time there was a little girl called . . .' goes Mummy. She is reading to me, but I don't know what she is reading.

'I think you need a second opinion. You need a specialist. It baffles me.' Dr Barker is in my room, his dark shape and his black bag are next to me. He goes out and I hear his voice going down the stairs. My head feels like the top of a bus with a man smoking cigars. A man did that once. I see his clouds of smoke. They are big, they hang above me like sponges. My arms and legs are enormous. I want to be sick.

Now there is another man in my room. A smaller man than Dr Barker. He is crouching down in the corner of my room and he is shining a torch in my eyes. Why is he doing that? Blinding white torchlight is in my eyes. Then it is gone and it is dark again.

Why do I feel sick? Read to me, Mummy. Read to me.

She is reading. She is there. She is gone.

It is daylight. I can see sunshine through the curtains. It's a nice day.

I try to sit up, but I can't. Never mind that, I'm really hungry.

Mummy comes tiptoeing into the room. She has her worried face on.

'Mummy,' I say. 'I want fried egg on fried bread. Now.'

Mummy sits on my bed. She is crying.

'Of course, darling,' she says. 'I'll get it straight away.'

What was she crying for? When I have had my fried egg, I shall get up. I want to look out of the window. I lie there thinking how nice it is not to feel sick any more.

Mummy comes in with a tray. I hadn't realised how good a fried egg on fried bread tastes. I shall have it every morning for breakfast now.

Mummy sits on the bed, watching me eat. She is smiling.

She takes the tray off the bed and puts it on the chest of drawers.

'Mummy,' I say, 'I want to look out of the window.'

She moves the bedclothes off me, but it is difficult to swing my legs out of the bed. She puts an arm round me and helps me up, but I can hardly walk. How peculiar this is. I need Mummy to get me across the room. And whose legs are those, moving down there? Those tiny, white matchsticks? They are not my legs. My legs are thicker than that. Surely they are not my legs?

But they are my legs. My new, stick-like legs that won't move properly.

Muriel Newmarch, aged 5 in 1908

Muriel's first attempt at a fashionable fringe, circa 1920

Muriel at school circa 1910 (centre)

Laurence Miles on The Picnic,
early 1920s

Muriel on The Picnic

Tea in the Garden, 1924. Laurence and Muriel at top of table

Laurence and Muriel wed, 1927

Judith at Broadstairs, aged two or three, 1938/9

Judith and Brother John, circa 1941 (about the time of the egg-throwing incident)

Judith at Sixth Form College,
Berkhampstead, 1954. Judith
second right

Judith aged 15, 1951

Muriel and her sisters, Norah and Mollie

The perky trainee teacher. Judith
aged 17, 1953

A very unsuitable boyfriend, 1953

On holiday in Majorca with unsuitable boyfriend, 1956

Daddy (on left) with work
colleague, circa 1958

Judith in BBC days, 1962

BBC staff training course,
1962 (Judith centre, back row)

Unsuitable husband, 1965

Daddy, Mummy, Brother John and Judith at John's wedding, 1966

Filming in 1972

Muriel 103rd birthday, 2006

Muriel's 106th birthday, 2009

Together Mummy and I get across the carpet to the window, and she picks up a corner of the curtain so that I can see the garden.

The daffodils are out. The last time I looked at the garden they weren't even showing through. But they're there. Golden faces nodding and a yellow sun. Yellow. All yellow. My favourite colour. Why haven't I seen the garden for such a long time?

'Oh Mummy,' I say, 'I nearly missed the daffodils, didn't I?'

Mummy is crying again.

'You nearly missed everything. That doctor thought you would die last night.'

'I didn't though, did I?' I say.

'I knew you wouldn't,' says Mummy. She laughs. 'Only the good die young.' She hugs me. 'My darling Doodie,' she says.

'Now the school wants us to fumigate all your books.'

'What's that mean, Mummy?'

'I have to put them in the oven and bake them.'

The daffodils are waving at me. Our cat is sitting on the concrete patch outside the French doors. But I don't think I can stand up much longer, even with Mummy holding me.

She helps me back to bed, and smooths the hair out of my eyes.

'You've had encephalitis,' she says. 'Daddy and I had never heard of it. We thought it was chickenpox.' She kisses my head.

'I'm going to bake your books now,' she says.

They come out of the oven brown and crisp like ginger biscuits. Mummy had the oven on too high.

We all laugh about that.

# The Egg-Cosy (1944)

I am doing my best stitching, but it's coming out big. This could be because I'm using a large needle – an embroidery needle, with red wool threaded through.

It is quiet in our kitchen. The boiler is glowing orange through its tiny windows. Gingerbread cottage windows they look like. Maybe there is a witch inside.

Our electric clock on the dresser says five past eleven. Mummy said she would be half an hour, so that means ... that means ... she will be back at twenty-five to twelve. Working it out should be easy but it screws my forehead up. Mummy says I am going to be useless at mental arithmetic, like Daddy. But he is very clever, I say. Not at things like that, she says.

If I look through the kitchen window I can see the snow is melting off the window-ledge. That means it will be slushy in the road and Mummy will have a wet, sloppy walk down to the chemist.

Mummy never leaves me on my own. Ever. But today she had to go and get some cough pastilles and cough mixture for my cold. She said I should stay indoors, and she has given me this sewing to do.

Our cat is curled on the rug in front of the boiler. He likes it there because it's cosy. I could kick my slippers off and stroke him with my foot – but I won't. He isn't as cuddly as he looks. In fact, he's bad-tempered – always ready to scratch.

Best to leave him alone. Mummy is disappointed in him. She likes a friendly cat.

I am wearing a Fair Isle jumper, a kilt and long woollen socks, and my bedroom slippers as I am staying indoors today.

Now I've gone all round the edge of this with red, I think I will go the other way with yellow. When it's finished it will be an egg-cosy. Mummy cut out this shape in pale green flannel from my old dressing-gown. I've grown out of it now. She's used up a lot of it already for covers for our stone hot-water bottles.

Anyway. I'm fastening off the red wool and cutting it with the scissors, so that I can go back the other way doing cross-stitch with yellow. It's good that this needle is an embroidery needle as wool is difficult to thread through an ordinary one.

I cut a length of yellow wool off and suck the end so that all the bits go together. The fibres I mean. Then I wind the wet end round the top of the needle and push the loop through the eye. Put a knot in the end and I'm ready to go the other way.

No noise – only the faint clunking of the clock and a sizzling sound from the boiler. We aren't getting air-raids every morning like we used to. It feels safer. It was bad last year. I got caught in an air-raid with Roger from my class. Roger likes me because I am the cleanest girl in the school, but that's not why we got caught in the air-raid.

The siren went off just as I got to school, so we had to go into the downstairs cloakrooms. And this air-raid went on and on. Ten o'clock, eleven o'clock, twelve o'clock – still going on and all of us sitting in the downstairs cloakrooms. Then people's mothers started calling at the school for them to take them home for dinner. And my mother didn't. And Roger's mother didn't. So we both decided to run for it. To run home, to our mothers.

(Ouch! I have just pushed the needle into my finger.)

Outside there was gunfire – there were bangs and explosions everywhere. In the sky there were shell-bursts and diving aeroplanes. And I felt very unsafe indeed. Roger met his mother on the way, but I didn't meet mine, and when I got home, no one was in. I went next door instead, and they were kind to me and gave me milk and biscuits, until I saw Mummy coming up the hill with my brother – and she was obviously in a state. Because she had called at the school for me and no one could find me. But it was all right in the end. Although I don't want to be outside in an air-raid again.

I have left a tiny spot of blood on my sewing. From pricking my finger. But I don't think it will show.

Now it is twenty past eleven. Mummy said that by the time I had finished the sewing she would be back.

Crumpet stretches himself out suddenly, in the glow from the fire. His whole black furry body goes stiff – his back legs shoot out like sticks and his front ones reach for the fringe of the rug. With his eyes tight shut, he looks as if he is smiling that secret cat smile they have. He makes a chirrupy half-complaining, half-contented noise. He's a misery, but I'm glad he's here to keep me company.

Bother. Now I'm going to sneeze. I put down the sewing and fumble in my navy blue knickers for my hankie – a big one of Daddy's. It's already soggy so it feels uncomfortable on my nose and it's pretty uncomfortable up my knicker-leg as well. I sneeze and sneeze into it. It will have to go in the laundry.

Half-past eleven. I am nearly at the end of the yellow stitching. Crumpet is now sitting bolt upright thinking about lunch.

*Tap, tap, tap, tappetty tap*. Footsteps coming up the hill. Definitely Mummy. I know Mummy's walk. She always wears shoes with a heel – even in this weather – and they make a tapping noise. Hurrying, busy, must-get-there sort of footsteps. It can't be anybody else. *Tap, tap, tappetty tap*. Getting closer.

I finish the yellow stitching and cut the wool. I put the needle in the needle case and the pieces of wool and the scissors back in Mummy's sewing basket, and look at my work.

It's definitely an egg-cosy. A pale green egg-cosy, with gigantic cross-stitching all round in red and yellow and a tiny bloodstain at the bottom.

*Tap, tap* down the front path. Mummy's key is in the door. The electric clock says twenty-five to twelve; Crumpet stands up arching his back.

I feel a cold draught as the front door opens – it is proper January weather outside. The warmth returns as the door closes and Mummy comes into the kitchen in her camel coat, shopping basket on her arm.

'Look,' I say. 'I've finished it.' I hold it up for her approval.

'Lovely, darling. Well done. That will be useful.'

I sneeze again, getting my wet hankie to my nose again.

'I need another hankie,' I say, dropping the damp ball on the floor.

'I tell you what,' she says, picking it up between finger and thumb. 'You go back to bed and I'll bring you a clean hanky of Dad's and something on a tray – and the cough pastilles.'

Sometimes it really is worth having a cold.

# Clothing Coupons (1945)

The school in my bedroom is busy. I have two dolls and a teddy sitting on the floor and my blackboard is up on the easel. Chalk at the ready. They are going to learn to be better at arithmetic than I am.

But Mummy is interrupting it all. I had closed the door, as I did not want to be disturbed, but here she is, opening it, rushing in, holding something in her hands.

'Look what I've made you!' she says, and lays whatever it is on the bed.

I walk over to see, and she holds up something in grey. Grey flannel. It's boys' stuff.

'A lovely pair of shorts!' she cries. 'I cut down an old pair of Daddy's trousers, so no need for clothing coupons.'

She dangles them at me.

'Don't you want to put them on?'

Not really, no. Why would I want to wear boys' stuff?

I don't say anything, but start pulling my dress over my head. It gets stuck.

'Undo it first, silly!' she says, reaching over me and getting at the two buttons behind my neck. She pulls the dress off, turning it inside out as she goes, putting it on the chair by the bed.

Now she hangs the shorts in front of me, encouraging me to step into them.

I hold onto her shoulders as I go, first one leg in, then the other – careful does it – and pull them up round my waist. They fasten with two hooks and eyes.

'They look really good!' says Mummy, all enthusiastic.

But I know they don't. I know from the feel of them, from the look of them as I peer down at my lower half. They are straight. They are grey flannel. They are boys' stuff. I don't want to look like a boy. I want to look like a girl.

'I won't wear them!' I say.

'Sssh – don't shout. Keep your voice down,' she says. 'Why ever not? They are lovely, smart little shorts. I took a lot of trouble with them.'

'NO! NO! NO!' I shout.

'But what's wrong with them?' she asks. She is upset. Well, she will just have to be upset. I didn't ask her to make them for me.

'They don't stick out!' I roar.

'Judith, darling, please. Be quiet. Stop this. What do you mean, don't stick out? They aren't meant to stick out. They're shorts.'

Yes, but even shorts can have a bit more material in them. So they look like a skirt. These look just like what John wears to school with his belt with the snake buckle. How can I convince her I will never, never, put them on? She can ask and ask and I won't. She can dress me in them forcibly and I will take them off.

'Go and look in the long mirror in my bedroom, darling,' says Mummy. 'You'll see how smart you look.'

I turn on my heel and go out of my bedroom and into hers next door. She hurries after me looking worried.

I open the polished mahogany door of the wardrobe – the left-hand door has the mirror in it – and turn round to face it. There is a small figure reflected and it is me in my vest wearing an ugly pair of grey-flannel trousers – straight, tight and stopping at the knee. They are awful.

I am so upset I drop to the floor and roll around in disappointment and grief. 'NO! NO! NO! Don't make me. Mummy, please let me go and take them off. Please let me! Don't make me wear them!'

Mummy has her head in her hands, her fingers in her ears.

'What's going on up there?' calls my father from the kitchen.

'Don't, oh don't go on so,' says Mummy. 'It's all right. I won't make you wear them. Do get up, and please *keep your voice down*!'

She goes out onto the landing.

'All right, dear,' she calls down. 'Only our daughter getting a bit out of control.'

'*Your* daughter,' says Daddy from the kitchen. '*Your* daughter has not learnt the meaning of the word "restraint".'

I get up off the floor and walk back into my bedroom – my pretty bedroom with the blue curtains. Blue utility material with animals. Mummy used my wooden Noah's Ark animals to cut out the shapes from khaki stuff and stitched them all round the bottom in a frieze. She is good at sewing but I wish she hadn't made these shorts.

I take them off and throw them on the bed. Then I reach for my dress from the chair and struggle into it. I don't do the buttons up at the back as they are hard to get at.

Mummy comes in looking beaten and tired. She starts doing up my buttons for me.

'Judith, there's a war on,' she says. 'Don't you realise how hard it is to get you clothes nowadays? *I* never minded wearing Mollie's things – or Norah's – when I was your age. I used to wear a lot of cut-downs and make-dos.'

She picks up the shorts from the bed. She holds them out, looks at them, her head on one side.

'It's not that,' I say, going back to my easel and picking up the chalk. 'It's the *shape* they are. All tight and boy-like. I want them fuller, so they stick out like girls' things. It's not *fair*.'

'But you can't get the material,' she wails, folding the shorts and hanging them on her arm. 'You need clothing coupons. We've used all ours up for this year. Anyway, whatever made you think that life was fair?'

I sit down suddenly on the bedside chair.

'How will I get a tutu for the ballet exam, then?'

'What do you mean?'

'I have to have a proper tutu and everything. You know I do.'

This is tragic. I am close to tears again.

Mummy stands, one hand on her hip, the other holding the shorts. She looks concerned. She has a nice face, my mummy, but she looks worried all the time.

Then she walks over to me and strokes my face.

'I remember,' she says. 'And I remember how I was going to do that for you.'

'How?' I ask.

'I shall cut up my wedding veil,' she says, going out of the room.

So that's all right then.

# The War Is Over (1945)

I went to Brownies last week and Brown Owl said the war was over and they weren't having a meeting that evening. She said to go home, so we did.

I walked back with Patricia, both of us in our brown uniforms with the yellow tie thing in the front. The reason I wanted to be a Brownie was so that I could wear this uniform. I'm not keen on some of the things we do though, and I failed one of the badges because I didn't know how to work out which direction was north. And I failed another one because Tawny Owl said that to lay a table properly you should turn the glasses upside down. Mummy was livid when I told her that. She said I had done it right and turning glasses upside down when you lay a table is common. Who is this Tawny Owl, she said? How dare she tell you to do something like that? Whatever sort of home has she come from?

Patricia's house is on the way to mine, and she asked me in to play with her new doll. But I said, 'No thank you,' because the last time I did that she said, 'I'll let you hold her for one minute,' and gave her to me and said, 'One,' and took her back again. I said, 'That's not fair – that was one second, not one minute,' and she said that was what she had meant anyway. She calls this doll 'Precious' and she has golden hair and eyes that open and close and eyelashes as well. Patricia's father is captain of a merchant navy ship and he got the doll for her somewhere abroad. I have never had a doll like that. No one could buy dolls in England during the war. You couldn't get them, like you couldn't get bananas. Patricia's father brought bananas home once – but they were dried ones and squashy.

Mummy says Patricia is not a nice little girl. Mummy says she is spoilt and nasty behind your back. She probably is – but she's the only other girl in the class who is clean and tidy like me. Except for Jean Broadhurst, although she wears ankle-strap shoes and Mummy says they are common.

So I went straight home and Mummy was surprised to see me. She had made some proper lemonade with lemons and sugar and I had a glass of that and a Lincoln Cream biscuit before I went to bed.

I like Jean Broadhurst's ankle-strap shoes and I want some. I wish they weren't common. I would like to learn tap-dancing like she does, but that is common as well, so I go to ballet classes instead. Which is nice, although I would love to have some tap-dancing shoes – shiny and tied on with a bow.

But a funny thing happened this morning. There was stuff in the newspapers about people called 'The Jews' and how Hitler had treated them badly and killed them. I asked Mummy, 'Who are these people called Jews?' and she said, 'They were the people who killed Jesus Christ and they deserve to suffer. God has said that they will always suffer, so that is why that happened to them. No question.'

She always says 'No question' when there are lots of questions.

I felt angry. I said it wasn't fair. I said the people who killed Jesus were hundreds of years ago and these people are now and they couldn't have had anything to do with killing Jesus so it was rubbish. And she said how you could always tell if someone was Jewish because of the shape of their noses and the way they talked. She said it as if being Jewish was something to be ashamed of and I didn't like it. I felt uncomfortable. Why should there be these people I am supposed to dislike? They haven't done anything wrong. I said that, but she said, 'Don't be silly, dear, you'll be late for school.'

So I am thinking about it. Being common. Being Jewish. Why should any of it matter?

# Let's Run Away (1946)

I don't think Mummy would like it if she knew what I have just done.

I shall put my hands behind my back and walk downstairs as if nothing has happened – I might sing a little.

I am on our landing, outside my bedroom door, and my bedroom door is shut. I think it's about five o'clock. Well, I'm sure it's about five o'clock because Dorothy came round for tea at half-past three. I can hear Mummy in the kitchen, running the water in the sink for the washing-up and walking backwards and forwards from the dining room clearing out the tea things.

It's summer – there is bright daylight coming through the frosted glass of the bathroom window in front of me. There is a lot of time left to play in the garden before bedtime – it stays light very late now. That's good. But I have a problem – and the problem is behind me, in the bedroom.

It's not my fault, though. Dorothy isn't really my friend. Well, she is, but Patricia is my Best Friend. Dorothy just tags along.

Sometimes when all three of us are walking home from school, Patricia puts a hand up and whispers in my ear. She says, 'Let's run away from Dorothy,' and she smiles as she takes her hand away, and then she nods, and glances at Dorothy, and looks back to me.

So we both run, as fast as we can – across the park, over the humps that were air-raid shelters, past the bottle factory and round the corner into the churchyard, where we can peer out and see what Dorothy is doing.

As I run, I often look behind me and I can see her, lagging a long way back, dragging her shoe-bag. She always looks as if she is crying. I tell Patricia, 'I think she's crying,' and Patricia laughs.

When we get to the churchyard, we look through the iron gates and watch her walking past with her head down and her nose running.

I don't like doing it much, but Patricia does, and I would do anything to please her because when she's pleased she's such fun to be with.

'Judith, what's going on up there?'

Mummy has noticed that I am missing and that it's very quiet. She is calling up the stairs.

I say, 'Nothing' – but it's not true.

The thing about Patricia is that it's all right when we run away from Dorothy, but it isn't nice when she and Dorothy run away from *me*. And that does happen. Not very often, but it happens, and then I am the one lagging behind, crying and feeling left out. So I know how it feels, and I know it isn't a good feeling. But I knew that anyway.

I think Patricia makes me behave badly. I'm nicer than she is. Mummy says I am. She doesn't like Patricia.

There is a muffled noise behind me and a lot of banging.

'What on earth is all that noise?' calls Mummy.

I need to sing to cover it up, so I go downstairs, humming very loudly. I hum along the hall and into the kitchen, and I stand at the door humming, with my hands behind my back.

Mummy has seized a drying-up cloth and is polishing away at one of our bread-and-butter plates. She looks at me, as I stand there humming.

'Where's Dorothy?' she asks.

'She had to go home,' I say.

'Had to go home? Without saying goodbye?' says Mummy, surprised. She puts the plate down on the kitchen table and pushes her hair out of her eyes. 'Do stop that humming,' she says. 'It's getting on my nerves.'

So I stop and we can hear the banging again. And a muffled yelling.

Mummy comes towards me and takes hold of my arm. 'Judith,' she says. 'What have you done? Where is Dorothy?'

I reply, 'She had to go home early.'

'Judith, that's not true, is it?' she says.

I always tell Mummy the truth and she knows that. So now it's getting awkward.

The family cat winds round my legs, quivering. He thinks it's suppertime.

'Look,' I say, 'Crumpet's hungry.'

'Keep to the point,' she says. 'Where is Dorothy?'

There are more cries and thumps from upstairs.

'I locked her in the toy cupboard,' I say.

Crumpet jumps up onto the kitchen table, and sits there, tail curled round, looking at us.

'Crumpet!' says Mummy sharply. 'Get down from there. Bad boy!' But he remains, fixed, looking at her as she flaps her hand at him.

'You've done what?' she says to me. She looks worried.

'I locked Dorothy in the toy cupboard,' I say.

'Oh, Judith, how could you? What a dreadful thing to do! What possessed you?' says Mummy, pushing me out of the kitchen, grabbing my hand and running up the stairs with me.

We reach the landing and the banging and crying is very loud up here.

Mummy opens my bedroom door, pulling me in behind her.

'Open the door,' she says, pointing at the toy cupboard. I can see that the boards at the bottom of the door are beginning to splinter, because Dorothy has been kicking it so hard.

So I unlock the door, and Dorothy falls out, crimson and

tear-stained. And I feel ashamed. I don't know why I did it, except that I thought it would please Patricia to hear about it.

Mummy is putting her arm round Dorothy.

'Dorothy – Judith's so sorry. Would you like a mug of milk and a biscuit? Judith, how could you?' She says these things all at once, first looking at Dorothy and then at me.

'No, thank you, Mrs Miles,' says Dorothy. 'I want to go home!'

'Of course you do, after a nasty shock like that. I'm sure Judith was only playing, weren't you, Judith?' says Mummy, looking both ways at once again.

'I only meant it as a joke,' I say. But I didn't. I don't know what I meant, but I knew it wasn't funny.

Mummy is taking Dorothy down the stairs.

'Have you got everything?' she is saying. And Dorothy is saying that she has, and if you ask me she can't get out of our front door quickly enough. I would feel the same if I were her.

'Bye,' I call from the top of the stairs. 'See you at school Monday.'

But Dorothy has gone, and the front door has banged behind her.

And now Mummy is coming up the stairs and her face looks cold and grey like a frying-pan.

'What was all that about,' she is saying as she comes towards me. 'How could you do that to your friend?'

'She's not really a friend,' I say. 'Patricia thinks she's soppy.'

My mother's face relaxes and looks less taut.

'I might have known Patricia was behind this,' she says.

'Well, Mrs Thompson at school thinks Patricia and I have a beautiful friendship,' I say. 'She said so last Friday.'

Mother has got me by the arm again.

'Mrs Thompson is a silly, sentimental woman,' she says. 'Patricia is a bad influence on you, and the sooner she moves up to Scotland the better.'

She drops my arm, and turns and goes downstairs.

I'd forgotten Patricia and her family were moving to Scotland. I shall miss her, but I think it will make things easier all round.

# The Scholarship (1947)

'Are you listening to me?'

'Yes, Mummy.'

I am dipping soldiers into my egg. The best bit, where the yolk is sticky and runny – and bright orange. Not all boiled eggs have orange yolks, some are mimosa-coloured. I think it is the brown ones that have darker yolks, which is why I try to make sure that mine is. Brown. And speckled preferably. You can taste the speckling.

'JUDITH!' Mummy's voice has got loud.

I dip another soldier into the yolk. Mummy has boiled this egg just right. Sometimes she leaves it in too long and then the yolk is hard. She puts lumps of butter into it then, trying to fool me that the runny butter is runny yolk. But it's not the same.

'What?'

I put the yolky finger of toast into my mouth and look at her, while I chew. What can be so important?

'You haven't heard a word I've said. You're miles away. Why don't you try harder?'

'Try harder to what, Mummy?'

'To do better at arithmetic, for one thing. Mrs Jones says you will pass "if it's your lucky day".'

'Does she?'

'Yes, she does. And she means you could do it if you put your mind to it.'

Mother puts her hand up to her head and rests her elbow on the table. She does this when she is worried. But there isn't anything I can do about it. She worries all the time.

I spoon some more egg into my mouth.

'Oh do look what you're doing,' she says. 'You've dropped it down your blouse and it was clean on this morning.'

Up she gets, dashing to the sink, turning on the hot water and putting a teacloth underneath the tap, running back, pulling at my blouse and rubbing it with the tea-towel.

'Let me dab you. If you do this quickly enough it all comes out. Why are you so careless?'

I am not sure. Does it matter?

'Do you realise what will happen if you don't pass?'

Mother returns to the sink with the tea-towel and puts it on the draining board.

'Don't pass what?' The egg is finished. I turn the empty

shell upside down in the egg-cup and bash the top with my spoon. To save the drowning sailors.

The clock on the shelf above says quarter to nine.

'The Scholarship – the Eleven Plus. Whatever it's called.'

She comes back and sits down in the chair at the table next to me again.

'You will have to go to a secondary modern. One of those dreadful schools for stupid children. You shouldn't go to one of those. It would be quite wrong for you. No question.'

'Would it? What is dreadful about them? Why?' I am really interested to know.

But she isn't listening any more. She is all worked up.

'Do you realise that I wake up in the mornings with my fists tightly clenched, like this' – she holds her hands up to me, her knuckles white, her fingernails dug into her palms – 'like *this* – because I am so worried about you not passing?'

'Really?' I say. 'Mummy, is there any bramble jelly?'

'I *knew* you weren't listening. Don't you care?'

I don't answer. I don't understand what caring means, or what trying harder at arithmetic means. Everything at school is easy – especially those intelligence tests. But I don't like 'area sums'. How can a garden path have an 'area'? It's not a square or an oblong.

Anyway, I'll be sitting the Eleven Plus next week so it's probably too late to find out now.

Mummy has her head in her hands. Is it my fault?

# The Family Tree (1947)

She is measuring my hand up against hers.

We are in our dining room and it's getting darkish, although it is warm and we have the French doors open. Mummy's at the table, with her sewing basket and a pile of socks for darning next to it. I'm sitting on the pouffe at her feet, half looking out into the garden and half talking to her, and she has got hold of my hand.

'Dear little hands,' she says, in a sort of satisfied way as she spreads her palm against mine.

'My hands aren't as small as yours, though,' I say, making the comparison. 'My fingers are longer, and I'm thicker through this bit.' I take my hand away and feel across the place where my fingers meet the back of my hand.

'A bit broader. Yes,' says Mummy, her head on one side, looking at her hands, and then at mine.

'But you've got lovely, filbert nails,' she adds.

'What are they?'

'You know how some people have stubby fingers and square nails?' she says.

Like Michael Armstrong's at school, I suppose she means. And Mavis Barnard's.

'Well,' she continues, 'yours are almond-shaped, like mine. Filbert.' She spreads her hands out on the table, looking at them. 'It's a sign of good breeding,' she says contentedly.

She picks up one of the socks and puts it on her hand,

squinting to see where the hole is. She finds it and pokes her finger through it, waggling it back and forth at me.

'Really?' I say. I am all ears.

'Oh, yes,' she goes on. 'You can tell people from good families by their hands.' She peels off the sock, and starts searching in her work-basket for the darning wool and the 'mushroom'.

'Our family goes all the way back to William the Conqueror,' she says. 'That's why my name is Newmarch. After one of the generals who came over in 1066. He headed a march up north I believe. So he got the name Nova-Marche. Sir Bernard de Nova-Marche. There's always been a Bernard Newmarch in the family. Uncle Dick's got the family tree somewhere, and eventually Cousin Bernard will have it.'

She finds the wool, the darning needle, the wooden 'mushroom' over which the sock fits while you darn, and her minute silver thimble. The only thimble small enough for her tiny finger.

'Are we aristocracy, then?' That would be romantic. Something special.

'Not really, darling. Not now anyway. Maybe once. All my family were younger sons of younger sons.'

'What does that mean?'

'The younger sons of aristocratic people went into the army or the Church.'

'Your father wasn't in the army, though. He was a bank clerk.'

'Thread this needle for me, darling. You know I can't see when the light starts to fade.'

She passes me the wool, the needle and the scissors. I suck

at the wool frantically and wind it round the top of the needle to make a flat loop. How I always do it. It's easier to get through the eye then.

'Yes, but *before* that, I mean,' she says. 'My mother and father were what they called "Reduced Gentlefolk". They met at St Anne's School for the Children of Reduced Gentlefolk at Redhill. I thought you knew all this. I've told you about it before.'

She has put on the thimble, and is wriggling a sock over the 'mushroom'.

'What was *his* father, then? And your mother's father?'

'Mother's father was an artist – a painter. Though not a very good one. He didn't earn much money at it. Thank you, dear.'

She takes the needle with the darning wool threaded through it.

'And my *father*'s father was a civil engineer and built bridges in India.'

I am curious.

'What did he look like? Did he look like you? Is there a photograph?'

Pulling her glasses down from the top of her head where they have been perching, she squints at the sock and starts darning, pushing the needle through the knitted heel, then pulling the wool through over the hole.

'Something happened to him.'

'What sort of thing?'

'Well . . .' she pauses, screwing up her eyes and peering at her work. 'Well,' she goes on, 'he got on board the ship in Bombay but he never got off at Southampton.'

I am aghast.

'Why, Mummy?'

She puts the darning down on her lap, and looks at me.

'What we used to say at home was, "Did he fall or was he pushed?"'

She resumes the darning, while I take this in. There is a whole story here.

A slight breeze comes in through the open French doors, making the little hairs on my arms shiver. I hear the electric clock's whirring ticking noise. A moth blunders in from outside, heading for the lamp.

Mummy bends her head, looking sideways at her work. She is making a web with the grey wool now, as the needle goes under, up, over and through.

'The Newmarches have a coat of arms, you know,' she goes on.

'Were Daddy's forebears aristocratic as well? He's got nice hands.'

'Of course not,' she says sharply. 'His grandfather on his mother's side was a fishmonger and on the other side he was an unpholsterer. Mind you, he had a contract to upholster the seats in all the London theatres, so he wasn't hard up. Until he drank the profits.'

'Is that why Daddy always says that his coat of arms is two kippers crossed on a field of upholsterer's webbing?'

Mummy puts down her darning and laughs.

'Does he say that? I didn't know.'

She stretches her feet out in front of her and turns one foot.

'See that high instep?'

'What's an instep?'

'This bit on the top of your foot. Mine is very high.'

I look. I suppose it is.

'That's another sign of good breeding,' she says. She puts her feet down and turns her chair towards the table to get on with the darning.

The moth is flapping about inside the lampshade.

I stretch my feet out in front of me, heels on the ground, toes up, in my socks and Clarks sandals.

'My insteps are not like that.'

'No,' says Mother. 'You've got your father's feet.'

# The First Day at the Grammar School (1947)

Mummy, Mummy, all the new girls were lined up inside the front door, in a corridor. We were leaning our backs against the wall – the wall was brown shiny tiles and the corridor floor was grey-and-blue-patterned stone flags. There were about five of us at first, but more and more came until there was quite a crowd.

Then a lady came through the front door in a long brown mac, flapping round her ankles. She had flat sandals on and no stockings so her bare toes were sticking out like a monk's. Her hair was a terrible mess – all straggly round her face and not a scrap of make-up on. She had a hooky nose and a string bag. I thought she was the school cleaner, I really did.

But then they came and took us to our classrooms – all along this corridor and down steps and round corners. And I was put in a classroom with THREE F on the door, and I sat at one of the desks – they were double desks, so we sat in twos, but I was on my own at first, because they kept bringing new girls in.

And these new girls had to stand in front of the class and the teacher said, 'This is WHOEVER' to us, and then she said to the girl, 'Is there anyone here you know?' and if there was, then the girl went and sat next to the person she knew.

But guess who the teacher was? The lady who had come through the front door looking so untidy and who I thought was the cleaner!

She had a lovely, educated voice, but she looked a sight. The outfit she had on under the awful raincoat was even worse than the raincoat. Sort of dreary beige colour and there were spills down the front.

There are about twenty-seven in my class. I don't know all their names yet, but they all seemed nice. Oh, and guess what, Mrs Salmon's daughter Barbara came in, and had to stand at the front of the class, and the teacher said, 'Is there anyone here you know, Barbara?' and she said, 'Yes, Judith,' and so she came and sat with me.

Why are you looking cross? Barbara is a nice girl, Mummy.

Well, I don't care if Mrs Salmon is your cleaner. Barbara has got to the grammar school with me, so it can't be helped.

What do you mean, you have got me to a good school and I have to fraternise with your cleaner's daughter? It wasn't my fault Barbara said she knew me. And anyway, what's wrong with Barbara? What's wrong with Mrs Salmon, come to that?

I know there's a nice girl you saw cycling past our house this morning wearing the school beret and you hoped I would get to know her and be friends with her. Perhaps I will be friends with her, but for now I shall be friends with Barbara because she sits next to me.

All right, so Mrs Salmon says toilet and pardon. Barbara does too, I expect. Why should that matter? Look, I don't especially want to be friends with Barbara, but if I did the fact that she is our cleaner's daughter would make no difference.

What's wrong with doing cleaning for a living?

Not the same class? What does that mean?

Why do you always say 'No question' when there are loads of questions?

I'm going upstairs. LEAVE ME ALONE!

## April Knows Everything (1948)

Mummy's friend is coming to tea today. Her name is April, which is a beautiful name. Much nicer than, say, June. Although June is a month name as well, and June is supposed to be better than April, because in April it rains. '*When April showers, may come your way . . .*' I sing under my breath.

I am helping Mummy polish the silver on our kitchen table.

We have sheets of newspaper spread out in front of us, and all the knives, forks, spoons and teaspoons are laid on them.

She has the polish stuff, which she is putting on with a cloth, and I have a clean duster to rub everything up bright and shiny. Mum is sitting in one of the kitchen chairs and I am on the stool, with the floppy cushion on it.

The polish leaves a sort of pink coating on the cutlery that dries and flakes. Like the calamine lotion Mummy put on my sunburn last summer. Perhaps it *is* calamine lotion? No. It's got a pungent, petrol-like smell.

Anyway. As I rub away I wonder why girls aren't called 'March', or 'February'. And no one I know is called 'July' – although I believe 'August' is a man's name. Why? Could you call a girl 'August'?

'Oh, Judith, do keep your mind on what you're doing,' says Mummy from her side of the table. 'You've left this serving spoon smeary. Look at it.' She picks it up and waves it at me. 'Do it again, and try to keep awake. Please.'

Our kitchen door is open and I can hear gardening noises. Someone, somewhere is mowing their lawn, and I can hear a chinking as my father digs the earth outside, turning it over with a fork and picking out the stones. And sawing is coming from the back garden of Number 19, three doors away. Mr Johnson is always sawing. I'm not sure what he is making, but it keeps him busy.

I say, 'Sorry, Mum,' and rub at the serving spoon with my duster until the smeary look goes and the metal gleams through. It's quite a pleasant process. And you can sit down to do it, which means you can think about other things.

Clink, clink, goes Daddy in the garden. The birds chat away. And then – that strange summery sound that comes and goes so quickly. *Rarely, rarely, comest thou, spirit of delight . . .*

The cuckoo. Faintly. Is it? Is it the cuckoo, calling warm days and my birthday?

It is. It is being borne on the wind across our garden and in through our back door. I put the spoon down, and sit, transfixed. Mummy is doing the same. We hardly dare to move, in case the spell is broken. In case it isn't true. In case it is just one of the wood-pigeons.

*Uh-oo . . . uh-oo . . . uh-ooh . . .*

Not a wood-pigeon. We strain to hear it. But it stops. It has left us with just the gardening noises and the sparrow chit-chat.

'First one this year, Mum,' I say, picking up a dusty, pink-covered teaspoon, and applying my cloth to it. 'What time is this April-person coming?'

Mummy gets up and reaches over the table for the cleaned cutlery, takes a fistful and goes out through the kitchen door and round into the dining room, where I hear her opening the drawers in the sideboard.

Suddenly the serving-hatch doors in the wall beside me are pushed aside and her face looks through.

'I've told you. About quarter to four – give or take. And she's not coming on her own. She's bringing Cedric with her.'

She turns away and goes back to the drawers, pushing the cutlery into all the right places.

'Who's Cedric?' I call through the hatch.

'Her husband. She should never have married him, of course.'

She turns back to the hatch, bending slightly to speak through it.

'Hand the rest of that stuff through to me, dear. And do

buck up. We haven't got all day and you've still got the forks to polish.' She stretches her arms through the opening, and I gather up the shiny spoons and knives and put them into her hands.

'What do you mean "shouldn't have married him"?' A bit of gossip. This sounds interesting.

Mother is rattling the cutlery into the drawers, but she calls over her shoulder, 'She should have married Bill.'

'Who's Bill?'

I hear the drawers being shut, as I finish my polishing of the forks, and Mother returns to the kitchen, going to the stove to put the kettle on the gas.

'Childhood sweetheart,' she says, fiddling with the gas tap and the matches. 'Damn this thing – why is it so difficult to light? Ah. Done it.'

She blows out the match and drops it in the waste bin, and positions the kettle over the flame.

I push my polished forks towards her.

'So why did she marry Cedric, then?'

'Money,' says Mother. 'No question. She was out for the main chance really. That was what April was like. Always was. I blame her mother.'

She picks up the forks and trots back into the dining room, rattling the drawers again.

I get up and peer through the hatch after her.

'Why did you like her, then?'

'She was fun,' says Mother, closing up the drawers. 'Always gay and pretty and flirtatious. Lots of fun.'

She turns from the sideboard and says, 'Are you going to help me lay the table and put the doilies out for the cakes? Oh, and the little cake forks you've just polished? Then we'll have a cup of tea and a quick lunch and be ready for them afterwards.'

We do all this. Daddy comes in from the garden and washes the grime from his hands under the kitchen tap. My brother drifts in from wherever and we have the quick lunch promised. Daddy offers to wash up and mother refuses. This is because Daddy takes two hours to do washing-up, as he has to sort everything out first into large plates, small plates, glasses, knives, forks, saucepans and miscellaneous. Then it has to be done in strict rotation: glasses first, then forks, spoons, large plates, small plates, followed by knives and saucepans, and by the time he has done that it is the day after tomorrow.

And April and Cedric are coming today. There is just time to change from messy Saturday-morning clothes into something better when it is 3.45 and I think they are knocking on the door. Someone is, anyway.

I sit in our sitting room, with my brother, looking at the jug of roses on the mantelpiece that Daddy picked this morning. The scent goes to my head, and I feel quite excited. I don't mind meeting new people, but my brother looks as if he would rather not be here, and Daddy has disappeared into the shed, doing something mysterious.

I hear the front door being opened, and voices in the hallway, and something about let me take your coats, and here they are. April and Cedric.

And April is beautiful. Her golden curls cascade round a heart-shaped face and a cherry-lipsticked mouth. On top of the curls perches a fuchsia-pink hat with a pink spotted veil. Very smart, I think, but a bit dressy. She smells of something nice but overpowering. Her figure is slim and beautiful in a fuchsia-pink suit – her nylon stockings glossy and her high heels peep-toed. Round her wrists jangle charm bracelets – maybe only one, but it looks like more. On the little finger of her right hand is a ring, with a dingle-dangle hanging from it. Her nails match her mouth.

And tall Cedric stands behind her, nervously, peering through horn-rims.

'This is my daughter,' says Mummy, waving her hand towards me as I get up to greet them.

April lifts her veil and I see her eyes. Green and cold as marbles, slightly popping out of her head. Glassy and sharp – boiled sweets, the sort that crack in your mouth and cut your tongue.

She looks at me with these terrible eyes and I know she hates me. She hates children and young people. She would rather we were not here.

But she tinkles. She doesn't speak. She tinkles. Like someone tapping a glass with a teaspoon.

'How lovely, Moo. A little girl. What's her name?' she asks Mother.

Why can't she ask me?

'This is Judith. And that is John,' says Mummy, as my brother gets up reluctantly.

April offers us her cheek.

'Cedric – say hello to John and Judith,' she orders as we kiss her powdery-pink cheek.

Cedric stands, rooted to the spot. He seems to have difficulty speaking. It is worrying. And then he says, 'Hel-hel-hello, John and J-J-Judith.'

Mummy makes them sit down and I think what an unusual way of speaking Cedric has. He does it all the time.

It is an awful afternoon. Even the little cakes with lemon icing that Mum made yesterday and I love, do not help at teatime. I don't like being with someone who doesn't like me. Not just me, but the very idea of me. It's obvious. And she doesn't like John much either, but as he is nearly fifteen I suppose he is not so much a child as I am.

The only interesting thing is Cedric's funny way of talking. I think I will try to talk like he does to cheer everything up. I hear the cuckoo again. Distantly.

So I say, 'L-l-listen. There's the cuck-cuck-cuckoo c-calling.'

No one responds. Maybe they haven't noticed my new way of speaking.

April tinkles away, and lifts the little finger with the dingle-dangle on as she sips her tea. Mummy has told me that is not a polite way to hold a teacup. She says it is 'genteel'. But she doesn't seem to mind April doing it.

And Cedric talks in his halting, funny way. Daddy says nothing. He hardly ever says anything when we have visitors – unless it's Auntie Norah. He likes Auntie Norah.

Mummy works away, talking like anything because no one else is.

I am relieved when they go. Daddy and Mummy stand in the hall and help them on with their coats, and April kisses Mum and says, 'Bye-bye, Moo; bye-bye, Laurence – mwah, mwah . . .' and Cedric calls, 'Good-bye, ch-children.'

'I'll give you a ring,' says Mummy. The door closes. And they are gone.

What a relief. But it isn't, because Mummy is steaming in

on me where I am sitting reading my book. She pulls the book out of my hands.

'Just what did you think you were doing, making fun of poor Cedric like that?'

'Like what?' I say.

'Imitating his stammer. It's an awful affliction. You musn't make fun of people who have things wrong with them. It's a dreadful thing to do. I thought you had better manners.'

'It was an interesting way to speak,' I say, leaning back in the armchair as she leans over me, all cross. 'I didn't mean to be rude. Is it an affliction? I didn't realise. I like copying the way people speak.'

Mother stands upright, looking at me, shaking her head.

'I couldn't help it,' I say. 'When I'm with people who speak in a particular way I copy them. I don't mean any harm.'

'All right. Keep your voice down,' says Mummy. 'I believe you. But try not to do it, because you can offend people.'

Daddy comes into the sitting room and takes out a cigarette from his case inside his jacket, tapping it on the outside of the metal to get the odd bits of tobacco out.

'Thank God they've gone,' he says, pulling his lighter out of his pocket.

'I don't like your friend April, Mum,' I say. 'She's got a hard heart. You can see it in her face.'

'April? Oh, she's all right,' says Mummy. 'My best friend. It's just that she's worldly-wise. And disappointed in Cedric. But she knows *everything*.'

My brother and Daddy and I look at one another.

# The Bust Bodice (1949)

I am in my second year at grammar school, and I have itchy stuff going on in the front of my chest. Things are developing. I didn't realise that developing things could be painful.

After my bath the other day, Mummy looked at my front in an appraising sort of way. Then she said, 'Yes. Your Brussels sprouts are coming on nicely.'

It was a joke. I once told her that someone at school called breasts 'Brussels sprouts'. That was OK. But Mummy using the term to me was not OK. I don't know why, but I felt embarrassed and interfered with. I didn't like her for saying that.

Anyway. I am sitting up in bed now, trying to get dressed. On my windowpane there is a grey etching, with tracery and fronds cutting deeply into the glass. Or that's what it looks like. I can't see through the window very well, because of the frost, but the roofs opposite look silvered over. An icicle is hanging down from the guttering above like the drip at the end of a nose. A seagull protests overhead. (Why? We are nowhere near the sea. Perhaps it's warmer here, inland.)

Getting out of bed on days like this is best avoided. But I've got to go to school, and Mummy is downstairs making porridge.

If you don't want to freeze as you put your bare feet to the floorboards the best thing to do is to get dressed *in* the bed. It's difficult, but it can be done, and I am doing it.

First you pull off your pyjama trousers and kick them down into the bed. Then you reach for your knickers on the bedside chair, drag them into bed with you and wriggle into them. You can do that with socks too, although you have to bend over a lot and sometimes it's hard to get them on straight and not twisted. After this you take off your pyjama jacket and you sit there feeling chilly. So you reach for your vest and your liberty bodice. Well, that is how it goes usually.

But today I have a new garment that must be put on before all those.

I pick it up gingerly and dangle it in front of me. I have never worn one of these before.

Downstairs I hear the pips going for the eight o'clock news. Mummy will be calling up the stairs any minute. She will be telling me to get a move on.

How do I start with this thing?

It is an ugly shade of pink in a shiny stiff material which I think is called bombazine. It has shoulder straps and lots of hooks running down one side.

'Judith! Are you ever getting up? Time's getting on,' Mummy shouts up the stairs.

I knew it. I can't take for ever sitting and looking at this thing.

Mummy bought it from the droopy draper's in the High Street. The sort of shop where they have vests and corsets hanging limply in the windows and advertisements for 'CHILPRUFE' everywhere. And knitted baby bonnets and socks. Where inside they have rails running overhead and little wooden cups with bills and money whizzing around from the counters to the cash desk.

Mummy says this thing is a Bust Bodice. She says I need to wear one now. She says I have a bosom and it doesn't look suitable on someone my age. She says thirteen is still a child.

I push my right arm through one of the shoulder straps and it hangs there for a bit. Then I push my left arm through the other shoulder strap and shrug the whole ugly thing onto my little pink breasts, bending my arms behind me to bring the back elastic round to the side where the hooks are. There are eight hooks to do up, and each one cuts into the soft flesh as I fasten it. It is an instrument of torture. I hate it. It hurts. It looks somehow surgical.

Little flakes of snow start hitting the windowpane. Maybe it will be too snowy to go to school today. Then again, I know that it won't.

'If you are not down here in five minutes there is going to be trouble, Judith. What *are* you doing up there? You'll be late for school like you were yesterday. No question. Now buck up.'

So I put on my vest over the horrible pink thing, and then the liberty bodice, and finally swing my legs out of the warm bed into the cold bedroom.

The rest of the dressing process has to be quick so I find my clean school blouse in the drawer, my gymslip in the cupboard and grab my navy V-necked pullover with the school colours round the edge to put over it all. Everything feels cold as I put it on. School shoes are somewhere. Ah. Under the bed.

I go downstairs to breakfast, and Mummy looks at my front again in that appraising way.

'Now *that* looks better,' she says.

# The Charleston (1950)

I am in the garden. Not the garden where the lawn and the flowers are, the top bit of the garden with the rockery and the crazy paving. The wild part, the part I imagine is my 'house'. Up by the fence is the patch which is my sitting room, along the path and to the right is the bedroom, and the small, scruffy piece where we buried the cat – and my doll – that is my kitchen. I am wandering around up here, going from room to room, imagining things. I am enjoying myself.

It is a Saturday morning in April, with a bit of a wind blowing, and the sun going in and out. Quite warm although I need my cardigan on. They must have the windows open next door, because I can hear their radio. *Housewife's Choice* it is – I know the opening music.

I look at the rough ground where the bones of our cat lie. I don't mind the thought of Crumpet under there, but the idea of my broken doll with no back to her head is upsetting. Once when Daddy was digging here he unearthed a pair of goo-goo eyes, covered in mud. They were only glass eyes, but I can't forget it. Her empty, broken skull and her unseeing eyes.

'You know Mrs Johnson at Number 21 asked me if there was anything wrong with you, don't you, Judith?'

I look up. Mummy has arrived – spoiling my peace. She is carrying a gigantic wicker basket full of clean washing, and dumps it on the paved path beneath the washing line.

I am still standing by the burial ground.

She stoops and starts pulling clothes out of the basket, draping them over the sides.

'Did she? What did she mean by that?'

Mother pulls two pegs off the line and puts them between her teeth. Then she bends and picks up a shirt from the basket and pegs it on the line, taking first one peg and then the other out of her mouth and fixing first one shoulder, then the next to the line.

'She's seen you, from her back windows, wandering about up here. She wondered if you were all right in the head.'

'It's my pretend house,' I say, walking over towards her.

Mother is bending over the washing again, sorting through it.

'Yes. I told her you would be doing something like that.'

'Does she think I'm potty? Really?'

Mother stands up with another shirt over her arm.

'No. Not now. I said you were just very imaginative.'

'Am I?'

'Dreamy, more like.'

She clamps two more pegs between her teeth and hangs out another shirt. 'Lovely day for the dry,' she says, tugging at the bottom of the shirt.

I stand by the basket, under the line.

'What's that mean?'

'It's what people say. Some people. It means it's good weather to hang your washing out to dry. A bit blowy and some sunshine. Are you going to stand there looking dopey, or are you going to help me with this?' She bends down to the basket again and pulls out a sheet.

A sheet. I know what that means. I have to help her fold it

double before we hang it on the line so that it catches the wind and billows like a sail.

Next door are boiling up something disgusting for their cat. I can smell it.

'Come on,' says Mother. She is holding up one end of the sheet already. The other is still in the basket so I bend down and fish it out.

'Hold it properly,' she orders. 'One hand *there* and the other one *there*.' She nods at the two corners.

I move my hands along to the ends of the sheet.

'Go back a bit,' she says, 'I want it straight.'

So I move back, holding the sheet, and Mummy moves back a bit as well until the sheet is stretched out between us.

'OK – to me—'

We move together in the old minuet we have done before, until my end meets hers and she takes it and throws it on the line, holding it on with one hand while she fumbles for the pegs with the other.

Next door's radio is playing 1920s dance music. *DAH, dah, DAH dah, dah dadidddy DAH dah* . . . It's a tune I know.

'Help me,' she calls, struggling to keep the folded sheet on the line. 'Stick a couple of pegs in up that end.'

As we fight to control the sheet, the next door's music gets louder.

'That's a tune I recall from my youth,' Mummy says, and starts humming it as she puts the last peg on the line. DAH dah, DAH dah . . .

She waves her arms about. Then she starts kicking out her legs and bending her knees – very quickly, while still waving her arms about.

'DAH DA DIDDY DAH dah—' she goes.

'Come on – you do it too!' she says to me, still whirling.

'I don't know how to do it,' I say, standing forlornly by the washing basket.

'It's only the Charleston,' she says. 'It's easy. Watch me.'

She slows down, turns and faces me, bends her knees and kicks a leg out.

'DAH dah,' she says.

I do exactly what she does.

'DAH, dadiddy dah dah,' she goes, doing the movements quicker.

I do them too. And, magic! Suddenly we are both dancing the Charleston in the vegetable garden, under the washing line, round the plum tree and over the dolly's grave – round and round, in and out, while next door's radio thumps out the tune.

I am amazed how my legs are going, and how I am whirling, looking up at the clouds as they blow across the sky, with the daft music pounding in my ears. It is easy. Mummy is right. And it's really good fun.

A blaring chord from next door's radio ends the music. The announcer's voice comes on, although I can't hear what he is saying.

Mummy is laughing, as she comes to a stop.

'I haven't done that for a while,' she says, picking up the last few clothes from the basket. 'Here, you peg these out for me while I go and clean the silver.'

She picks up the empty wicker basket and walks away from me, towards the house.

'Why do you have to clean the silver?' I call after her. '*Again?*'

'Because it needs doing *again*,' she says. 'And that's before I wash the cushion covers and start getting lunch . . .' She hurries off, and I hear her doing her sing-song chant, 'Never-be-done, never-be-done, never-be-done . . .' as she goes.

If I had a real house, instead of a pretend one, I don't think I would spend all my time cleaning it, like she does.

I peg up the last few handkerchiefs and socks she has given me, then tilt my head back to look at the sky again. Little muddy clouds float across it. It is the colour of my doll's eyes.

# The Best of the Day Will Have Gone (1951)

Mother is hoovering the stairs. She has the hosepipe attachment fixed to the vacuum cleaner, and is on her knees in her overall, halfway down. In her free hand is a duster for getting into the corners that the hosepipe thing can't reach.

I know all this because I can hear her, and this is what she always does on Mondays – rain or shine. When she's done the stairs she'll do the hall, then the sitting room and the dining room, and while she does it all she will chant her sing-song tune, 'Never-be-done, never-be-done, never-be-done . . .'

Mother is what might be called 'house-proud'. Only she would call it 'Having Standards'. High ones – higher than they need be. I don't think it's necessary to keep a house spotless; a house is for living in, not for polishing.

It is April – the Easter holidays.

Father is in the garden making sure the edge of the lawn is absolutely straight, using long-handled shears to trim the stray bits of overhanging grass.

I can hear a blackbird singing on a branch through the open window; inside the light goes up and down as the sun moves in and out of cloud. The first roses are in the stone pot on the mantelpiece. The hands of the electric clock are at 11.15.

My brother and I are curled comfortably in separate chairs in the dining room, reading. He is reading something by Fred Hoyle, and I am consuming Mazo de la Roche, *Return to Jalna* – fantastic. Another world.

Which suddenly explodes. Mother is in the doorway, duster in hand, scarf round her head, rubber gloves on.

'What are you doing snurging in here?' is her first remark.

She walks swiftly across the room and snatches John's book from his hands.

'Just look at the weather!' she cries, waving the book at the window.

She turns on me now. 'And you're as bad! As bad as each other you are. No one else is indoors on a day like this. What *is* the matter with you both?'

She walks towards me, and takes Mazo de la Roche away from me, putting both books down on the dining-room table.

'Can I just finish that chapter?' I plead.

*SNIP, SNIP, SNIP* goes my father's strange long-handled gardening tool.

'No, you cannot. Go for a walk or go and help your father in the garden. One or the other. Don't sit in here all morning.'

My brother and I exchange glances. Not much good offering to help Daddy – he has no idea of delegation and hates being interfered with when he's gardening.

'Where shall we go?'

Mother has started dusting the dining-room table now – lifting up the books and rubbing around under them.

'I don't care. Just go for a walk *somewhere*. I don't understand you, John,' she says to my brother. 'You need the sun for your spots – it will do you good to get outside in the fresh air. No question.'

She starts on the bookcase.

I wince. My brother hates being reminded that he has acne. Why can't she understand that?

We stand, undecided, deprived of our reading matter, looking helpless.

'Go *on*. I don't want to see you back here till lunchtime. Now *move* – or the best of the day will have gone.'

The Best of the Day Will Have Gone. The ultimate failure. Somehow to miss this moment of splendour – whatever it is exactly – is to be an outcast from civilised society. In Mother's scale of values.

There is no peace, when our mother is around. You cannot hide away with a book, or your thoughts; you have to be Out, making sure you do not miss the Best of the Day.

My brother and I have nicknamed her 'The Dreaded Mum'.

She has whizzed out of the room, duster in hand, and up the stairs, to bring the hoover down and start on the upholstery in the sitting room.

'Do we need our coats?' we ask after her.

'Need your coats? Of course not. If you weren't so dopey you would know that,' she calls from the landing.

She is staggering down the stairs, hoover and flexible attachment under her arm, duster in her teeth.

We stand in the hall, looking at her.

She plonks the hoover down and removes the duster from her teeth.

'*OUT!*' she orders.


# Fifteen (1951)


I am wide awake and it is 1.15 in the morning.

I was fifteen last week. Sweet fifteen. But I am fat.

I don't feel fat, but at school they bracket me with the others who are tubby. Or tubbyish. Jean Draper, Sylvia Gerrard (although I can't be as fat as she is, she is a complete barrel), Evelyn Hayes. But Evelyn is enormous. She's tall as well as big.

Then again, my brother teases me.

I suppose I could tease him about his spots, but the thing is, I mind less about being fat than he minds being spotty.

I would like, more than anything, to be a normal size like

everyone else. So that, when Mummy takes me clothes shopping and says, 'Have you got anything to fit this young lady?' the sales assistant won't look me up and down, purse her lips and draw in her breath while she shakes her head.

We went to buy school knickers yesterday – navy blue interlock – and Mummy asked whether they had any in my size, and the lady brought out a pair and spread them on the counter and said, 'These have just come in, Madam. Lovely, aren't they? Aren't they big?' And Mummy looked at me, trying not to laugh, and we bought two pairs and walked out of the shop saying, 'Lovely. Aren't they big?' to each other.

I don't like lying here, awake, thinking these thoughts. I don't like to think I'm fat – but worse than that, I think I am mentally ill as well.

I have these funny feelings. Not funny feelings – scary feelings. Sometimes I feel half of me detaching and watching me and I can't get back into me again. It frightens me. There is this dreadful mental illness called schizophrenia and it affects adolescents. Obviously that is what I must have. People commit suicide if they have it – or they murder their parents. What would happen if I murdered my parents? In the night – not knowing about it – while I was being this other person?

Then again, there was this thirteen-year-old girl who had such a shock when her dog ran across the road in front of a bus that she dropped dead. You can drop dead from shock – I didn't know that. That could happen to me. It could happen *at any moment*.

This is awful. I can feel my heart beating and beating – soon it will stop. It's bound to. It stands to reason. In fact, I can't understand why it doesn't stop now.

I moan with fear, and curl up into a ball in the bed, sobbing with fright.

But the door opens and Mummy creeps in.

'What *is* the matter?' she whispers. 'You'll wake everyone up. Keep your voice down.'

'I'm going to die!' I say.

'Of course you are,' she whispers. 'One day. Everyone does. Move over.'

She climbs into bed beside me. It makes it very crowded, but she is only tiny so there is just room.

She puts her arms round me and cuddles me as if I was still a baby.

'Shh,' she says. 'Tell me all about it.'

So I tell her I might be mad. I tell her all about schizophrenia.

'Darling, there is no insanity in our family,' she says.

'What about Daddy's mad aunts?'

'They weren't mad. Just eccentric. There's a difference.'

'Are you sure?'

'Absolutely. No question.'

Very distantly the church clock strikes the half-hour. It feels wrong being cuddled by your mother at half-past one in the morning when you are fifteen. I'm not quite comfortable with it.

'Is that all you were worried about?' she asks.

So I tell her about dropping dead suddenly.

And she laughs. Mummy, who is always so worried about me, she laughs.

'Oh you are silly,' she says. 'I'm quite sure you aren't going to die – not until you are old. Don't you think I would be concerned about you if I thought it was likely?'

'Yes.'

'And do I seem worried?'

'No.'

'There you are then. People who drop dead suddenly have got things wrong with them. Our family haven't got anything wrong with them. Strong hearts, strong lungs – strong everything. Mother's sister Florrie lived to be 101 – and Mother would not have died at sixty-two if she hadn't had such a hard life. And look at your father's mother. Nanny's alive and kicking, driving us all dotty, at eighty.'

She holds me tight.

'Do stop worrying about nonsense,' she says. 'There are so many real things to worry about in life. These are sick fancies. So stop it, and go to sleep.'

But I am so relieved at what she has said that I am falling asleep in her arms.

I feel her wriggle out of the bed softly, and tiptoe to the door, closing it gently behind her.

But it still feels wrong to be cuddled by your mother when you are fifteen. Especially when you are twice as big as your mother. Sometimes I feel like a cuckoo in a sparrow's nest.

# Nice in a Lot of Ways (1952)

Three years ago we bought this nice house – a big one, with four bedrooms. I've never lived in a four-bedroomed house.

Three bedrooms was what we always had before. So this house feels massive. It is spacious and airy and has high ceilings and a long garden that goes on for ever and has interesting tangled bits down at the bottom.

I'm sitting on the sofa in the big bay window with the French doors open, looking down the garden now.

Mum loves this house. She says it is the first house she has been able to choose without Father interfering and going all over it doing his surveyor stuff and saying it's not suitable because it's got subsidence, or a crack under the lavatory window or a problem with the roof. She says we have always lived in houses she hated but that were a good proposition as far as the survey went. In other words, had passed Dad's tests. But this one they both liked and Dad didn't find anything wrong with it structurally at all.

So we moved in, and my grandmother moved in with us. She has the fourth bedroom to herself, as a bedsitting room, and has brought lots of interesting stuff with her. Her room is different from the other rooms in the house. A different world – a much *older* world. I love going in there. And I love Daddy's mother. 'Nanny' we call her. She wanted to be called that. Mummy is supposed to call her 'Mother Miles', but she doesn't. The only time 'Mother Miles' is used is if she signs a birthday card or a letter to Mum. Sometimes she just puts MM, which means 'Mother Miles'.

Nanny has really beautiful, sloping handwriting. Old-fashioned, with pothooks. But very elegant. She writes lovely letters. I like getting letters from her.

When I was tiny she used to sit me on her mattressy lap and tell me this silly story I loved. It went 'Once upon a time there was a teeny-tiny old woman, who lived in a teeny-tiny house with a teeny-tiny front door . . .' She used to say this early part very quietly, and I would stare into her face as she looked down at me. I could see the powder on her cheeks and smell her lavender water as she went on, looking at me steadily. 'One day the teeny-tiny woman put on her teeny-tiny coat and her teeny-tiny hat and went out for a teeny-tiny walk . . .' 'Did she go through her teeny-tiny front door, Nanny?' 'Of course. And she went up her teeny-tiny front path . . .'

On and on it went, in Nanny's quiet voice, until the teeny-tiny old woman had found a teeny-tiny churchyard and a teeny-tiny grave with a teeny-tiny bone lying on top of it. And taken the teeny-tiny bone back to her teeny-tiny house, of course, and up her teeny-tiny stairs to her teeny-tiny bedroom. And after she had put on her teeny-tiny nightdress and got into her teeny-tiny bed and blown out her teeny-tiny candle she lay there in the dark and heard a teeny-tiny voice saying, 'Give me back my teeny-tiny bone . . .'

By this time my eyes would be out on stalks and I would be gripping Nanny's arm waiting for the best bit. Then she would whisper . . .

'And the teeny-tiny old woman said – *TAKE IT!*' The last two words were bellowed so that I fell off her lap in delight and terror.

I lean back on the sofa, still looking out at the garden, because I am thinking. Wondering why having Nanny here is not as nice as I thought it might be.

Last night we had sausages for supper – and Nanny had fish. Mummy cooked it specially. Nanny doesn't like meat. She says when she was little she used to faint at the sight of raw meat because she was delicate. And sensitive. So she always had fish or cheese instead. She eats very slowly so meals take a long time, and she doesn't hear what anyone else is saying, which is OK as she likes to do all the talking anyway. And she rattled on.

'I was only talking to Mrs Sterry yesterday about this, Muriel. I said to her, I said, "Muriel feels exactly the same as I do . . ."'

'No, I don't. I don't agree with you.'

'Yes, Muriel agrees with me. I told her that.'

'But I DON'T!'

'So I told her, "Muriel agrees with me." That's what I said.'

Afterwards she put on a big pinny and stood between Mummy and the sink saying, 'Now dear, what can I do to help?' and I could see Mummy trying to dash round her with the dirty plates and get on with everything so that she could start the ironing.

'Nothing, dear. You go upstairs and have a little sit-down in your room.'

But Nanny doesn't sit in her room. Hardly ever.

I like going in there, though. I look at all her old photograph albums when I am up there – with pictures of her when she was young, and Daddy when he was a big fat baby and Aunt Winifred in a frilly pinafore, and lots more. And then, best of all, there are the bound copies of *Punch* from 1875 up to 1930. I love those. There is a marvellous 1870s cartoon of a fat lady trying to get into a cart, with the driver looking over his shoulder saying, 'Try sideways, Mrs Jones, try sideways.' And the fat lady is saying, 'Lor bless 'ee John, I ain't got no sideways . . .'

Then there is the 1930s one showing a very modern, fitted kitchen – co-ordinated units all round – and a maid in a frilled apron and cap standing in the middle of the floor saying to a lady in evening dress, 'Please, Mum, I've put the dinner in somewhere and now I can't find it . . .'

It's social history.

But Nanny didn't sit in her room last night. She sat with us reading Mummy's library book, while Mummy did the ironing in the kitchen. And when Mummy finally came in, Nanny said, 'There you are at last, dear. I expect you'd like to sit down and look at your book.' And she passed the book over to her.

Mummy took the book and collapsed into an armchair with it.

'I don't think you'll like it much, though,' said Nanny. 'You know that nice young man in chapter 3? Well, he dies in chapter 10 and it's no good after that.'

And today Mummy isn't dashing round doing all her usual things – dusting, hoovering, washing – 'never-be-done, never-be-done'. It is very quiet everywhere, for a Saturday. Daddy has gone to the library, and, for once, Nanny is in her room. I can hear her creaking overhead, but I can't hear Mummy.

I get up from the sofa and wander into the dining room, wondering where she has got to.

And she is in there, sitting on one of the small armchairs, pulled right up in front of the fireplace. She has lit a little fire. In June. A few sticks and some newspaper and a tiny, flickering flame in the blackened grate. She is pulling the chair nearer and nearer the fire, and she is shivering.

'Mum,' I say. 'Are you all right?' I walk over to her.

She looks at me. Her face is grey.

'I'm so cold, dear,' she says.

I kneel in front of her and take one of her hands. It is freezing.

'I don't think I can go on,' she says. 'With Nanny here. She's always in my way. She towers over me. She won't stay in her room. She's taking over.'

She bends her head and her shoulders start shaking. She looks up at me, tears running down her face.

'And it's so difficult for me, with your father not speaking to her.'

She huddles down as if she is trying to warm herself.

'No one should have to ruin their life looking after an elderly relative. It's not right.' She shivers again and looks at me with her grey face.

'She'll have to go and live with her daughter,' she says.

'But Winifred hates her.'

'Even so.' She shakes and shivers again. I take her other hand. Cold as a frog.

'Winifred's awful to her, Mum. She said she didn't know why she wouldn't die. She said, "Other people's mothers die – why don't *you* die?" You know she did.'

'Yes. Poor Nanny. That was a dreadful thing to say. Still, Nanny's *her* mother. She's not *my* mother.'

'So why doesn't Daddy speak to her when she's here?'

'I don't know,' she whispers. 'Some small, silly thing she did to him when he was a child. You know how he is.'

I hear Nanny's door opening, and her heavy, slow tread on the landing.

'She's coming downstairs, Mum.'

'I can't talk to her. Take her out for a walk, Dood. Somewhere. Please.'

I scramble to my feet.

'*I've* always liked her,' I say.

'Yes,' shivers Mummy. 'She is a nice person. She's very nice. Very nice in a lot of ways. But not to live with.'

My grandmother's steady, slow, measured step is on the stairs. Her large frame fills the dining-room doorway.

'Now, dear,' she says loudly. 'What can I do to help today?'

'Nothing,' says Mummy. 'Dood's going to take you for a walk, and I'm going to go up to the doctor's, aren't I?' she says, looking at me.

Nanny moves slowly towards us and stands over Mummy's chair.

'Going to the doctor's?' she says loudly. 'Whatever for, Muriel?'

# Going Shopping (1953)

We are off to Oxford Street for the day. Mummy and I, jogging along together on the tube to Tottenham Court Road.

Mummy has a large bag with 'John Lewis' on it on her lap, so we look as if we have already been shopping – which we

have, in a way. Last week. This is a different kind of shopping.
This is Taking It Back shopping.

The carriage is not particularly full because it is 10.30 in the
morning, so all the business people have already got to work.

The train swings along, going round a bend. I can't see the
bend, because we are in the tunnel, but I can feel it. And all the
straps that you hang onto if you can't find a seat are swinging
backwards and forwards down the middle of the carriage.

Mummy is wearing a short camel coat and a navy blue
beret. She always wears a beret – and so do Aunts Norah and
Mollie. It's odd seeing them out together in their camel coats
and berets. They look like triplets, although it has to be said
that they made these choices independently and without consulting one another. Just funny how their similarities show
themselves.

I look down at our feet, neatly positioned on the wooden
floor. I am wearing my first pair of Cuban heels, and Mummy
has on her usual medium stacked-heel shoes that she wears for
pounding the London pavements.

The man and woman sitting opposite are both reading
books. They are about middle forties, and look strikingly
alike. They do not speak to each other.

Suddenly Mother's mouth is in my ear. 'Do you think those
two are married? Or brother and sister?' she hisses.

The train bursts from the dark into the daylight, briefly,
before plunging back into the tunnel.

'Married,' I say, into the hair beneath the beret on my side.

'Mmm. Can't be sure,' she replies, looking at them curi-
ously.

The train slows down as it comes out of the tunnel into the

lights of a station, then grinds to a halt. There is a jolting noise and the doors slide open.

The man opposite looks up, closes his book, rises and dashes out of the doors just as they are closing. The woman continues to read her book.

'Wrong on both counts,' I whisper to Mother.

As the train pulls out of the station she says, 'What station was that? Was that Goodge Street?'

'Yes,' I say.

She starts struggling with her parcel, her handbag and a small shopping bag she has with her.

'Come on then,' she says. 'Next station. Don't leave your gloves behind on the seat – watch what you're doing for good-ness sake.'

I'm not looking forward to the next few hours. My mother has endless energy for charging in and out of big stores, up and down in lifts and round and round display rails which I don't share. It's very tiring, and she never wants to sit down and have a coffee or go to the loo.

'Good heavens, dear, we haven't time for that,' she always says.

The train comes to a stop once more, and we stumble out onto the platform looking for the Way Out. As usual it is as far away as it can be down the platform. We trudge towards it and I think of all the people who used to sleep down here ten years ago. During the war.

'It must have been very uncomfortable,' I say to her as we walk.

'What must?'

'Sleeping down here in the war,' I say.

'Yes – dreadful,' she says. 'A lot of people died once – at Bethnal Green, trying to get down to the platform when the air-raid warning went. Anyway, don't think about that. The war's over, thank the Lord.'

We haul ourselves and the big carrier bag to the escalator, standing looking at the posters on the wall as we go up. *Take it from me – Phillips Stick-a-Soles DOUBLE the life of your shoes!* The dependable cobbler with the greying hair and glasses beams at me as I pass him. My brother calls them 'Stick-Arseoles'. Next comes *If You Want to Get Ahead Get a Hat!* I think it should be the other way round: 'If you want to get a hat, get a head.' Obvious, really.

'What are you giggling at?' asks Mother as we step off the escalator single-file, and she takes my arm so we go two-by-two.

'Oh nothing,' I say, as we go out of the tube station into Oxford Street.

'Yes, it was,' she insists. 'It was something. Don't get like your father – telling jokes to himself that he never shares.'

'I was just thinking it ought to be, "If you want to get a hat get a head,"' I say.

Mother stops her trotting and stands in Oxford Street laughing. For a second.

'I think you *are* like your father,' she says, starting to trot again and pulling on my arm. 'But better, because you *talk*.'

She slips her arm out of mine and goes round behind me, arriving on my left side and taking hold of my left arm, swapping her carrier bag and handbag over as she goes.

'You know I like to be on the *outside* of the pavement, dear. It's a bit higher.'

'So?'

'Well, I look taller on this side. Now, best foot forward, it's quite a step to John Lewis.'

And so we go, at top speed, arm-in-arm, weaving in and out of the crowds, hopping across Oxford Street and balancing on what Mother calls the 'save-your-life' in the middle, while buses, taxis, cars and motorbikes all roar past, until there is a gap and we can plunge across the other half of the road and get onto the pavement again.

Mother pushes me ahead of her through the august portals of John Lewis, and sweeps me up the escalator to the Ladies' Fashion floor, where she pauses, holding her carrier bag and her handbag with the small shopping bag clasped before her. I stand next to her, as she scans the floor.

She spots a free assistant behind one of the counters.

'Over there,' she nods, and together we advance across the carpeted floor.

The saleslady, in black with a white collar, says, 'Good morning' to us, giving a friendly smile from a magenta mouth. 'Can I help you?' she enquires.

Adopting a confidential voice, Mother lays her John Lewis carrier on the counter before her, opens it up and offers it to the assistant.

'Well, I wonder if you can,' she says. 'I'd like to return this.'

The bag is opened and a grey dress is removed and shaken out. The saleswoman holds it in front of her, scrutinising it at arm's length – first one side, then the other.

Laying it down on the counter she looks at Mother and says, 'What is wrong with the garment, Madam?'

Mother's voice gets even more confidential and she leans towards her.

'Nothing is wrong with it. It's just that my husband doesn't like it. Won't let me wear it. He says he won't be seen with me in it.'

What a tragic story. My father wouldn't notice if my mother was dressed in a flour bag. I have to admire her narrative skill – she is an object lesson to me.

Mother looks downcast and apologetic.

'The receipt's in the bag,' she says. 'I do wonder if you would be kind enough to arrange a refund. In the circumstances.'

'Miss Jones!' calls the assistant to a tall grey-haired woman, also in black with a white collar, high-heeled black patent shoes and straight stocking-seams, who is passing. 'Miss Jones! Can you help, please?'

Miss Jones sails towards us, and stops by the counter, looking at us, from one to the other.

'Is there a problem?' she asks.

'Madam would like a refund on this, Miss Jones.'

Mother stands mutely, eyes downcast.

'What is wrong with the garment?' asks Miss Jones, inevitably.

'Nothing – but the customer's husband doesn't like her in it, Miss Jones.'

Other shoppers move across the floor and round the display rails. A woman slips into one of the changing rooms with a dress over her arm and an assistant following her. One of the lifts arrives opposite us, and two women and a pushchair get out.

We stand around the counter. Four of us. There is an appreciable pause.

'Of course, Madam,' says Miss Jones to Mother. Everything is now explained to her satisfaction. She smiles understandingly. She lifts her eyebrows. If the lady's husband doesn't like it there is no more to be done, the eyebrows say.

It is amazing to me.

'Please arrange a refund for Madam,' she says to our assistant with a nod. She casts off and begins cruising the floor again.

Mother digs her elbow in my side and looks at me.

'Shhhhh!' she hisses as the dress is taken away, the receipt looked at, and the paperwork attended to.

Fifteen pounds is eventually handed over to Mother, who stuffs it in her purse. 'Thank you so much,' she purrs. 'Now we can go round and look for something else.'

'Of course,' is the reply, with a wide smile of encouragement.

Mother and I leave her, somewhat lighter minus the carrier bag.

'I thought you were going to tell them that Daddy doesn't care what I put on,' she says, giggling.

'Well, he doesn't,' I say.

'No – but *they* don't know that,' she says, still laughing. 'Now buck up, I want to look at coats.'

'Can't we have a coffee and go to the loo?' I plead.

'Good heavens, dear – we haven't got time for that. What a girl you are, always wanting to go to the loo.'

She is bearing down on the coats section, with me in tow.

'Well, don't you?' I say.

'I'm made like the angels. You know me. I shan't need to until it's time to go home. Probably not even then. Go on, if you must. I'll be here, looking at the coats. But buck up.'

She is already absorbed in the rails, with other customers. Two ladies dressed in black with white collars stand by the changing rooms, hands clasped in front.

'Can you ask someone if there is a Petite section?' she calls over her shoulder as I go towards the Ladies.


## Seventeen (1953)


Today is my seventeenth birthday and the weather is cele-bratory. I don't remember such a sunny day for my birthday before. Perhaps that's because I never felt so happy before. Which is why I am writing up my diary – something I hardly ever do, as nothing happens. 'Forget what did' is hardly worth entering. Not like all this.

Only two years ago I was a fat fifteen-year-old and dotty – well, I thought I was. But now I know I'm sane. Clever, even – although I don't bother much at school. Better than all of that, I am slim. I have a 23″ waist and I only weigh 8st 3lbs. And I look good. I have to keep staring at the mirror to make sure it's me. But it is.

All my brother's friends are hammering on the front door these days, wanting to take me out. That's a laugh, because they've known me for ages – right through my tubby, childish phase, and they weren't hammering on the door then. So it goes to show the perfidy of men. You can't trust them. You are the same person inside but you don't look like Brigitte Bardot – they don't notice you; then suddenly you *do* look like Brigitte Bardot (a bit – if I put my hair up in a chignon) and they're all over you. What does that say about them?

But maybe I'm not the same person as I was at fifteen. I was half asleep or something. My headmistress told my mother that I had had 'a very heavy adolescence' – whatever that means.

But today I met someone. A boy. He had a lovely voice and freckles and a lock of hair that flopped over his face and got into his eyes. I met him because I went down to the cricket ground with my friend Ann to help with the scoring. Ann has been doing the scoring there for ages. She is willowy and blonde and a bit vapid but she has loads of boyfriends because of the way she looks. And she meets them at this cricket ground.

Mummy had just finished making me a new summer dress – lavender-and-white-check gingham with lavender binding round the edges of the armholes and a lavender belt, plus tucks in the skirt going round the bottom a bit like frills. Nice swirly, gathered skirt exactly how I like it. I put that on, and some new white shoes with flat heels and bows on the front, and a bracelet my auntie Mollie gave me for my birthday made of china beads on a spring that went round my wrist with a bunch of china flowers on the top. I had never seen a bracelet like that before. Matching earrings too. And Nanny had sent me a five-pound note in a birthday card with her lovely sloping writing inside. So I was feeling rich.

'You look charming,' said Mummy, standing back and

surveying her handiwork. 'There is no doubt – you are a very pretty girl.' Then she smiled and nodded. 'I done you,' she said, half to herself.

And off I went to the cricket.

I felt great swinging down the road, knowing I looked good, with the sun burning the pavements and all the striped blinds down over people's front doors because it was hot. Faded, stiff canvas, most of them. Like the sails of old yachts.

I got to the cricket ground and met Ann. She took me up into the wooden box above the pavilion where the scorers sit. A fat, oldish chap showed me how to fill in the scoring book, and above my head was a roller-towel thing with numbers on it, which you pulled on to display the score. Filling in the scoring book was interesting. I had always thought cricket was a boring game (though aesthetically very pleasing *the plangent toc of bat on ball* . . . – gosh, who wrote that?). But if you have to analyse every ball and make a note of when a wicket is scored or draw in an M for maiden over and so on, you get involved.

Teatime arrived and some of the players came up into our box – *they* said they wanted to look at the bowling analyses but *I* think they wanted to see Ann. And one of them was this freckle-faced boy with the floppy hair and lovely thin hands and a voice like a Shakespearian actor. He said to me, 'Would you like a cup of tea?' So I said yes, and back he came with it and we talked. And he was interested in all the things I'm interested in – poetry and acting and painting, not just science, like my brother's friends – and he was interested in *me* as well. He gave me his phone number and took mine and wanted to know my name and where I went to school and all of that. He said he was an articled clerk with an accountant's office in Victoria and he was nineteen and had recently left St Albans School, which is a good boys' public school. His name is Tony. I have a Cousin Tony who is also handsome and charming. Maybe that name goes with that sort of person.

I shall tell Mummy, of course. I tell her most things. She'll be pleased as I think she worried I would always be mooning over unobtainable ballet dancers. She tried to get me to go out with soppy Geoffrey Broome once. She said, 'He comes from a good family.' I said, 'He's soppy and he wears a soppy white linen jacket.' She said, 'It's perfectly suitable – what's wrong with his jacket?'

She didn't understand that Geoffrey Broome makes my flesh creep. He put his arm round me in the cinema once and it was revolting. Then he wrote me a letter which began, *Dear Judith, I am exhausted – nay, knackered ...* Pretentious and pompous. And he enclosed a packet of stink-bombs he had made in his lab at Oxford. He thought it would amuse me. Everything was wrong with him.

But this Tony is lovely. I hope he rings me, or I shall cry.

# The Row Over Tony (1954)

'But he's nice. I love him. *You* like him too. Why shouldn't I go on seeing him?'

My mother and I are sitting in my bedroom on the floor in front of the small electric fire, with our arms round our knees. My face is a bit too close to the fire and feels burning hot. Things are going on in my head that feel like flames. Mother has lit them.

'I'm telling you to be careful. He'll break your heart.'

'What do you mean?'

'It's the sort of boy he is. Think what his father is like. Always after women.'

'You don't know that.'

'It's what Tony told you, isn't it? And he's the same. You can tell. The acorn never falls far from the tree.'

'This is all rubbish.'

'I don't want you to be hurt, darling.'

She wants to stop me having a life, she means. I get up and pull the curtains as it's getting dark outside. The window in my bedroom is a triangular bay, a lookout, with a wide triangular sill. Useful to sit on and watch what's going on in the street below. I draw the curtains together and go back to sit on the carpet in front of the fire with her again.

'You know what your father says about him?' she resumes.

'No. What?'

'He says, "That boy will either end up as prime minister or on the end of a rope" – that's what he said to me last night.'

'What did he mean?'

'He meant that Tony is good material but he is flawed. He is like a beautiful piece of china with a crack right down it. Then there's his awful sister.'

It is now dark in the room. The only light is from the two-barred fire. Our faces look shadowed and conspiratorial. I clench my hands together round my knees. This conversation is making me feel pulled in two different directions – and hot with the friction of it.

'Heather?'

'Yes, Heather, or whatever her name is. She looks down on us. She looks down on you. She thinks you are a boring suburban girl.'

'How do you know?'

'Because when she answers the phone to you she always says, 'Who shall I tell him is calling?' You told me she did. She *knows* who's calling. She just doesn't approve of you for her brother. I know I'm right.'

'Why would she not?'

'*Her* mother danced for Diaghilev, *she* went to RADA, *their* family is artistic and bohemian . . . ours is ordinary compared with that.'

'Yes, but their dad is a child-welfare officer.'

'He was an RAF hero during the war. And he's only a welfare officer now because he can't get another job as he's a drinker. That's what it is. No question.'

'Shut up.'

'I'm so worried about you,' she says. In the half-light I can see the creases and furrows in her face tightening. She has screwed her hands into fists. It annoys me.

'Why are you worried, for goodness sake?'

'I'm worried that his sister will cause trouble and *he* will break your heart. That he'll go off with someone else – just like his father has done. He's a playboy. You should finish it. Why don't you agree to a clean break?'

A crater yawns between us. White-hot anger spills.

'You don't want me to have any experiences in life, do you? You want to keep me in a glass case to which only you have the key so that you can see I am safe and not going to come to any harm!' I am shouting at her like Daddy shouts at her when she irritates him. And I can see why she does. And now I can't stop.

'Life is *about* coming to harm, finding out about stuff, getting hurt. You're selfish and possessive. You don't *own* me. I resent you trying to interfere in my life and "protect" me. I don't want to be protected. I don't need you to worry about me. Why do you always expect the worst? Stop going on.'

Now she is nearly in tears.

'I want your happiness. That's all. Mothers do. If you can say these things to me I no longer have a daughter.' She gets to her feet. She has her back to me. '"Sharper than the serpent's tooth is the ungrateful child,"' she says.

'You are an awful mother. I hate you. How dare you talk to me like this?'

'Like what? You are my daughter. You can say anything you like to your own daughter.'

'No, you cannot. That is exactly what you *cannot* do. You're wrong. I'm a person. I am not an extension of YOU. You are interfering and selfish.'

'And you are a bully.'

I don't care.

'I'm not some doll to dress and put back in a box when you've finished with me,' I yell, turning her round.

'You tower over me, and you dominate me. You bully me,' she repeats. 'Do what you like, Judith. Get hurt. Don't come to me and tell me about it, that's all. Just wait until *you* have a daughter.'

She has gone. The door has closed behind her. I sit down on the carpet again. I am alone by the electric fire. I put my arms round my knees and bend my head onto them. A blow for freedom. You have to strike them, or never grow up.

What's all this about being a *very ordinary* family? She never uses the word 'ordinary' except in a pejorative sense.

It's true his sister is a silly snob and very cold towards me. But how can she have these preconceived notions about me? She hasn't even met me. Why should Mother be so defensive on my behalf? Is there something wrong with me, then? Something I should worry about? Or is Mummy a silly snob too?

I don't care. Tony loves me. No one can come between us – not his sister, and certainly not my mother.

There is the other as well. The feelings that only I know about. Sex. It's nice. Nobody else has ever made me feel like Tony does. Trembly all over. I don't think my father ever made my mother feel trembly in her life. She doesn't behave as if she knows what goes on when two people get physical. Bet she's never had an orgasm – wouldn't know what one was. Though I suppose I have to blame Dad for that. Not that Tony and I have proper sex. Petting, the Americans call it. Sounds a bit like having a puppy dog – it's quite the wrong word.

I start remembering lying on my back under the trees in Hadley Wood with Tony's lovely hands moving over me and the shadow of the leaves rubbing back and forth above our heads. And him showing me what you do to kiss someone properly.

But Mummy's crying somewhere. I suppose I had better go and make it up.

# 'I've Found Out What Love Is' (1955)

The letter from Tony came for me this morning. It was in my college pigeonhole. There was the Basildon Bond envelope, with his lovely, flowing writing across the middle of it in the pale blue-black ink he uses. *Miss Judith Miles, Bognor Regis Teacher Training College, Sussex*, it read. His letters are usually very thick, but this one felt thinnish. All the same, it will be full of love – or maybe a suggestion that he comes down to visit me. It is in my pocket now.

Having a letter from Tony makes the day wonderful. I hear the wood-pigeons crooning, I notice the dew on spiders' webs – little things like that become big things. The colour of leaves is brighter, the prospect of the morning's lectures more delightful, my friends more interesting. Everything looks clearer and sharper. Breathless and waiting. All things are possible.

And joining the queue for college breakfast with his unopened letter in my cardigan pocket fills me with excitement. I think I will have the scrambled egg and the fried bread *and* the sausage this morning. I grab a tray and slide it along the counter, thumping my file of papers down on it.

I wonder what Tony will say? He will be loving – he always is. Although once he wrote that Mummy was a 'fire-eating, over-protective dragon, always looking for some hurt to be delivered to her child. If you look for hurt, you will find it.' Had her bang to rights, to be truthful.

The red polished floor of the refectory gleams, the lady serving up the scrambled eggs smiles and Denis Hubbard ahead of me turns and looks at me admiringly, one hand on his tray.

'You're looking extremely beautiful, this morning, Miss Trotty,' he says.

It's his silly name for me. 'Trotty Wag-tail'. He says it's the way I walk in my pencil skirt – especially noticeable from behind, he says.

I smile at him and indicate to the lady who serves the sausages that I would like two.

'Oh dear – you won't keep that lovely figure for long,' says Denis. 'TWO bangers. That's excessive.'

'Well, *you're* in no position to criticise,' I say, as we move to the coffee and tea counter. 'You've got bacon and two fried eggs AND fried potatoes. Plus you have a definite embon-point.'

'It doesn't matter for men,' he says, taking a mug of tea and turning with his tray to look for a table. 'It gives us substance.'

Rubbish, I think. But then I know he is only arguing for victory, like Dr Johnson.

We both find spaces at one of the trestle tables. Our refec-tory is in the crypt of an old church or chapel on the college site. The noise of conversation – knives, forks and metal plate covers clattering, and tea-urns sizzling, fills the air. I love it.

I have a plate of scrambled eggs and sausages, a mug of hot tea in front of me, admiring glances from the men and a letter from Tony in my pocket. Life is perfect. And I am wearing one of my new white collars that you put round your neck on top of your jumper and tie with a ribbon. I have put a black ribbon through mine, and I know it suits me. I laugh, I talk and I flirt because I am good at it. But all the time I am thinking of the letter in my pocket.

After breakfast we walk to our different lectures through the grounds. The training college is housed in three old buildings, one a lovely Regency house called The Dome and two more ordinary Victorian ones, The Shrubbery and Mornington House. I am on my way to Mornington House. There is a small man with a moustache called Bill walking with me. I thought he was a dead loss at first, but I am finding out that people are usually nice and often interesting in spite of the way they look. You have to be tolerant and not respond to prejudiced first impressions. And Bill is knowledgeable about birds, and worth listening to when he talks about his favourite subject. We are both hugging our files.

But I think now is the moment for me to read my letter, as I'm not really listening to Bill's conversation. So I put my file under my arm, pull the envelope out of my pocket, hold it with my teeth and tear it open with my spare hand. Then I get the blue sheet out and unfold it. One sheet. I try not to feel disappointed.

I look at the letter as I walk. Sometimes Tony illustrates the margins with silly, loving drawings. But he hasn't done that this time. And usually he begins *Darling Judith*, but he hasn't done that either. *Dear Judith*, it begins.

I think my stomach is going to fall out onto the path.

*Dear Judith,*

*I am sorry to have to write to you in this way, but I am afraid that I must. You see, I have fallen in love for the first time. Her name is Sally, and she is a friend of Heather's, and a bit older than me, which means she knows more about everything, if you know what I mean . . .*

My stomach has fallen out now. My hands sweat. My heart races.

*Sally is an actress like my sister, although at the moment she is working in the umbrella department of John Lewis. But that is only while she is waiting for a professional engagement. Her professional name is Sally Grace, but her real name is Sarah Potts.*

Bill is still chatting on. The sun is still shining. The birds are still singing. But the asphalt path on which we are walking seems to be coming up to hit me. Black, flat and heavy, it is punching me in the face.

*At last I've found out what love is. I don't think I knew before. So this is my last letter to you. I hope you will do well at college.*

*With best wishes,*

*Yours Tony.*

And no kisses. Of course, no kisses.

Why do I feel as if my legs won't walk?

'You OK?' asks Bill, looking at me.

I beam at him.

'Of course. Never better. Race you to The Shrubbery.'

Headless chickens, I have heard, run round and round the barnyard after decapitation. That is what this is like. Your outside goes running around as normal while your inside is dead.

But I shall ring Mummy tonight. I know what she will say. 'I *told* you he'd hurt you.' And if I cry, she will cry too – she always does. It won't help.

# Being a Secretary Is a Very Good Job (1956)

'Well, if you aren't going to be a teacher you will have to take a secretarial course.'

Mummy and I are in the coffee shop at Debenham & Freebody's. Dark polished wood is everywhere. The tables are dark and polished, the chairs and the panels round the room. All dark and polished. Discreet, quiet, and with very few customers.

It is a sunny spring day, but the outside light does not penetrate this sanctum sanctorum of the upper-middle classes. We have come here looking for shoes. Mummy has great difficulty finding these as her feet are tiny. Size three is hard to come by in shoe shops. She felt she might do better here, in a department store.

We have spent a frustrating morning sitting on plush chairs while an assistant brought shoe after shoe for Mother to try on.

'I like these. Have you got them in navy, in a size three?'

'One moment, Madam, I'll check for you.'

It was uncomfortably hot in the shoe department. I wriggled out of my coat and scarf, laying them on the empty seat beside me.

'Don't leave them there! You'll go and forget them. And do your handbag up. Everything's falling out of it.'

Once a mother always a mother, it would seem. Even when your daughter is twenty years old.

'We have them in a size four, Madam. Will you try them?'

Why would you want to try on a size four if your shoe size is three, I wonder.

We got through navy shoes in the wrong size, and black shoes, brown shoes and red shoes in the right size, until it seemed imperative to have a coffee and a sandwich. Something she rarely stops for, but shopping for shoes exhausts her.

'Being a secretary is a good job,' says my mother, stirring her coffee, and putting the spoon back on the saucer.

My heart sinks. It would be the worst job in the world. For me, it would.

'You could be looking after someone important – arranging his diary . . .'

She chats on.

Arranging His Diary would be awful. I don't want to be a dogsbody to some Important Man. Really. Arranging His Diary – there could be nothing worse.

My mother doesn't know me at all. She thinks I am like her. There is something in me she doesn't get.

A man in a trilby sits down next to Mother, removes his hat and puts it on the table beside him, while he consults the leatherette-covered menu.

'I've brought my poem for you to read, Mum,' I say.

'That's nice, dear,' she says.

I am proud of this. My first published poem in a 'Little Magazine'. I fish it out of my shopping bag, and lay it before her, open at the page.

She puts on her glasses, screws up her eyes, and reads it, half aloud and half to herself.

'Mmm; mmm; mmm; dah-di-dah and doo-di-doo . . .'

She takes off her glasses, closes the magazine and pushes it back to me.

'It's lovely, darling,' she says. She puts her glasses away in the case, snaps it shut and returns it to her handbag.

She pats my hand, and looks at me. 'My clever daughter,' she says.

I don't know about that, but I know I don't want to sit behind a typewriter somewhere.

Our sandwiches arrive and I pick up a knife and cut mine in half. I am hungry after all those shoes.

'I'll have the poached egg,' says the man next to us to the waitress, closing the menu.

Mother is rummaging – her head down, her hands ferreting away in her string bag. At last she brings out a copy of *Radio Times* and puts it on the table.

'Here it is. I brought it specially. See – here.' She swivels it round so that it faces me, pointing a finger at an advertisement she has circled in pencil.

'It says, "The BBC needs secretarial staff in all production departments ... dah-di dah ..." You'd like that, wouldn't you?'

Well, I might. But the secretarial course would have to come first – and the idea fills me with gloom.

'Are you thinking of Pitman's?' I mutter.

'Oh no, dear, nothing like that. Pitman's is common. No. There's a nice secretarial college in Great Portland Street we could afford to send you to.'

And only yesterday I was walking down Great Portland Street in my new high heels thinking that London was my oyster, with my two A Levels and my five O Levels and my one and a half years at teacher training college (Failed – Due to Walking Out With a Broken Heart Before Finishing the Course). I was thinking there was nothing I could not do. Seems I was wrong.

'You'll enjoy learning shorthand, dear. I did.'

Yes. But I want to be an actress. Or a poet.


## He's Not Suitable (1960)


'We don't like him, Judith. I think you should end it.'

The communal hall of the big Hampstead house in which I have a bedsitter is chilly. It's March, but they have turned the heating off already. I'm leaning up against the wall by the telephone, the receiver to my ear, listening as she goes on and on.

'You never like *anybody* I bring home, Mum,' I say. My feet are aching. I've had a long day at the office – not a hard day, just a long day.

'Well, why do you go for these people? Why can't you find a nice young man in a proper job?'

'There's no such thing as a "nice" young man, Mother. Trust me.'

'Of course there is. It's just that you aren't interested in them.'

'What do you mean by a "proper" job, anyway?'

I stretch out for the light switch. It is getting dark in here.

'I mean a sensible nine-to-five job. A young man who works in a bank. Or an insurance office. Something like that.'

'What's wrong with being a television set-designer?'

I manage to switch the light on, and the hall is illuminated in all its neglected Victorian splendour – high ceiling, black and white tiles, decorated mirror (like something out of a pub) and the stone staircase with the iron balustrade down which I have tripped to answer the echoing ring of the telephone.

'You know what I mean.'

I don't know what she means. But nothing is stopping her now.

'What happened to the nice chap from Standard Motors who took you to Paris? Now he was a nice young man. We liked him.'

'That nice young man, as you call him, wanted his wicked way with me as soon as we hit the Champs Elysées, and when he didn't get it he sulked and wouldn't speak to me for the whole weekend.'

'Really? Well, it must have been something YOU did for him to behave like that. No question.'

'He was looking for a wife, Mum.'

'What's wrong with that?'

'Looking for a wife the way he would shop for a shirt in Marks & Spencer. "This one's a nice colour – not too pricey – this'll do." I'm not going home with some bloke to be hung on a hanger – "Look what I got yesterday – nice, isn't it?"'

My feet are definitely aching now. Wish they had a chair here. I slide down the wall and sit on the cold tiles, still holding the receiver. This is going on and on.

'Well, this Ron, or whatever his name is, is a horror. When you brought him to dinner I thought, "What has she got hold of now?" He was the death's head at the feast. Had nothing to say to us. Seemed to think we weren't worth talking to. When he did talk he was condescending. And I didn't like the way he looked at you. He didn't look at you the way he should. I want to see you with some man who looks at you as if he cares about you. I know how I want a man to look at you, and he doesn't do it.'

I lean against the wall and close my eyes.

'Or what about that lovely man from the BBC Hungarian Section? With the melting eyes? Miklos someone or other? The son of the deposed minister for education? You know who I mean. Oh I took to him. He was a charmer – a real charmer.'

A real charmer. I remember him well. Used to call me 'little one' and was enjoying a bit of a diversion with me while running a full-time affair with a married woman. I ended up at a bus-stop in the fog where he dumped me as he was anxious not to be late for a tryst with her afterwards.

'I worry about you so much, darling. And I'm sure this Ron is quite the wrong person for you. I wish you would listen to me. But you never do. Your father didn't like him either.'

'Uh-huh—'

'You're not listening, are you? As I say, you never do. You must stop looking for Tony all over again. You won't find anyone exactly like him – and anyway, look at the way he hurt you. Better off without. That evening when you rang me about his letter, though – I knew, I just knew, something awful had happened to you. I felt it. I did, honestly. I felt it. Round about ten o'clock in the morning I thought, "Something dreadful has happened to my Doodie" and I was right, wasn't I? Mother's instinct, that is. You'll know when you have children.'

'Mmm—'

'Oh go away – you're not listening. Why do I bother? You worry me sick. You look so pretty now, but there will come a time when you won't and if you aren't careful you will be on your own when you are old.'

'Everyone's on their own anyway.'

'No, they're not. What do you mean?'

'Think about it.'

One of the other residents comes down the stairs, steps over me, and goes into the kitchen opposite. I get to my knees, still holding the phone, and pull myself upright using the banister head.

'Someone wants to use the phone, Mum. I'd better go.'

'Why can we NEVER talk?'

'We've been talking for half an hour and it's time I went and heated up my baked beans.'

'How can you eat those things?'

'Lovely. My treat. Now go away and stop badgering me.'

'Think about what I've said.'

'Yes, Mummy.'

'Just like you were when you were a child. "Yes, Mummy," you used to say – then you'd go and do exactly the opposite of what I'd asked.'

I've edged up to the telephone shelf now, ready to replace the receiver on the cradle. The metal fitment with the A and B buttons presses into my shoulder.

'Must stop now, Mummy. This other person needs the phone.'

The hall is empty. But I've had enough.

'I'll ring you tomorrow,' I say.

Yes. Right.

'Bye, Mum.' I put the phone down.

The other resident emerges from the kitchen with a tray and a plate of toast. 'Does she ever give up, your mother?' she asks as she goes up the stairs.

# Funny How Things Turn Out (1964)

I am standing by the open drawer of a filing cabinet in a small office in circular Television Centre. The architects were onto a good thing when they designed it doughnut-shaped – all fittings have to be custom-made to fit. Someone's making a big profit.

If I look out of the window I can see the naked, bronze figure of Ariel below, holding a clock of hours, surrounded by sea-nymphs. It should be a fountain but when the fountain is running it floods the editing suites in the basement, so it never does. Run. Bit of a let-down really as you enter the glamorous world of television. Without the water Ariel is getting scaly and covered in dried white patches.

I can see the bald head of the controller of BBC 2 crossing beneath me now, walking from reception to the side door to the studios. He doesn't give Ariel a second glance. None of us does. Part of the furniture Ariel is, with his dried-up nymphs.

'Time for my medicine, I think,' says the lady producer I am working with. She is sitting at her desk in the corner, peering at a handbag mirror and trying to adjust a multi-coloured scarf on her head with one hand. It is tied in a sort of turban. She pushes it this way, then that, frowning at her reflection. She looks up at herself under her eyebrows, pursing her lips.

'What *are* you wearing?' I ask her, as I take a file from the cabinet.

'My "arrangement",' comes the reply. 'Don't you like it? Didn't have time to wash my hair this morning.'

I think about my answer. 'It's quite striking,' I say.

'That's the point of it,' she replies, snapping shut the little mirror and pushing it into her bag. 'You coming to the club?'

She grabs her cigarettes from the desk, and gets up, making towards the open door onto the corridor.

'Yes – a bit later,' I say. 'I'll catch you up. Just want to do something here.'

She sweeps past me, holding on to her 'arrangement'. It wobbles as she goes – makes me think of Carmen Miranda.

I shut the filing cabinet drawer, looking round the open office door as she exits.

'What do you want to drink?' she calls over her shoulder.

'A red wine,' I call after her.

'Large or small?'

'What do you think?'

'Large then,' she says as she heads off down the corridor.

Peace descends. I lay the file I have taken from the cabinet on my desk and sit down on my chair to study it. I have been meaning to do this for a year.

A gaggle of secretaries swing past the door on their way to lunch, laughing and nudging each other.

'Are we going to the canteen or the salad bar?' asks one.

'Oh the canteen,' says another. 'We might see the *Z-Cars* cast . . .'

Their chatter fades.

The buff-coloured file lies in front of me. It is labelled AUDITIONS/INTERVIEWS; ACTRESSES: A–M: Jan. 1959.

What was her professional name? Sally – what was it? GRACE. Sally Grace. Knew it began with a G.

I turn the pages, going past the file-dividers – A, B, CDEF and now G.

This file was compiled years before I started working here – very neat and efficient it is, much better than anything I would do. Filing is not my forte.

I turn the sheets in the G section and there she is. GRACE, SALLY, with lots of handwritten notes on a printed form.

The telephone rings. Really annoying, just as I struck gold.

I glance at my watch. Five past one. I can guess who is ringing me. But I pick up the phone and say, 'Drama Serials' in an efficient voice. Just in case.

'There you are, dear,' crackles Mother. I needn't have bothered with efficiency.

'Where do you expect me to be?' I ask. 'At one o'clock on a weekday?'

'You'll never guess who I have just met,' she says.

'Go on. You're going to tell me anyway.'

The head of Drama Serials puts his head through the open door.

'Where is she then?' he enquires of me.

'In the bar, with a large vodka,' I say, removing the phone from my ear, one hand over the mouthpiece. Mother is quacking away distantly.

'A woman of taste and discernment,' he says. 'I shall join her.' His head is withdrawn and the rest of his besuited body follows as he goes down the corridor.

I put the telephone to my ear again.

'Did you hear what I said? You've gone away. Where are you?'

'I'm here. I am supposed to be at work you know – something came up.'

'Wasn't it extraordinary, though? Meeting him like that?'

'Who are we talking about?'

'Tony. That boy Tony. Would charm the birds off the trees. You know. Who broke your heart. As I knew he would.'

This is truly a coincidence.

'Never! Where? How? Tell me about it.'

'I've been trying to, darling. He came in half an hour ago. Into this office.'

My mother is doing a secretarial job in the West End, a post she achieved by dint of lying about her age. They think she is fifty-something. In fact she is over sixty. She has also worked in market research, using the same ploy.

A shirtsleeved arm drops an envelope into our postal 'In' tray by the door and withdraws.

'Why did he? Come into your office?'

'That's the extraordinary thing. He's an area manager for Olivetti typewriters, dear, and he came with a trainee, to try and sell us a typewriter – well, to show the trainee how it's done.'

'So he's not an accountant, then? Failed his exams, I suppose.'

'I don't know about that. But he's got married.'

Something sharp plunges in between my ribs. Ridiculous. It's been nine years.

'Yes – married. And his wife's expecting a baby. Her name's Emily, or something. No. Emma,' he said.

Not Sally then. So much for real love at last.

'Yes. Emma. They live in Stoke Poges.'

And leaves the world to darkness and to me.

'He was quite delightful to talk to. But then he always was.

I liked him a lot, you know. But not for you. And of course, his sister did her best to ruin everything. It would never have done. She found him that woman, that Sally. No question.'

I look at the open file in front of me.

'Funny you should say that, Mum. I've got some audition notes here. Seems the Sally woman came along looking for work a few years ago.'

'Oh how interesting. What do they say?'

'You do realise this stuff is probably confidential?'

'Don't be ridiculous. I'm your mother.'

I look at Sally's notes, reading them out into the mouth-piece.

'Height: 5'6"
'Age: 30
'Good speaking voice; a little too stiff. Reads expressively but does not take direction well. No TV experience. Stage: *Smiling Thro'* Watford Rep. Not v. useful. Keep on file possibly. Rides a horse. NG dialects.'

My mother is laughing.

'There – and you would have thought she would be taking the West End by storm by now,' she says.

It's not right to laugh. Actors have terrible lives – something like 30 per cent unemployment in the profession. And you have to remember what they said about Fred Astaire on his notes: 'Can't sing; dances a little'. All the same I'm glad she didn't get anywhere.

I close the file.

'You've got to laugh, haven't you?' I say to Mother.

'Funny how things turn out,' she says. 'But you could have knocked me down with a feather when Tony walked in. Area manager for Olivetti, indeed. He reckoned on being Chancellor of the Exchequer, didn't he?'

My other telephone is ringing.

'I don't think that *he* did, but I think his sister did.'

It is still ringing.

'Isn't that your other phone ringing?'

'Yes. Must dash, Mum. See you at the weekend. Byesy-bye.'

'Oh, why can we *never* talk?'

But I have put the telephone down. I let the other one ring. After all, it's lunchtime. They can call back. I've got a large glass of red wine waiting for me in the BBC Club.

# Find Someone With a Proper Job (1965)

'I've only called to let you know I'll be going away for a week. To Devon. With Alan.'

It is early morning in the office. Well, it is ten minutes to ten, but that is early for BBC Television Centre. No one gets in before ten, and most not until 10.30. In production departments. They get there earlier in Admin.

I am slumped at my desk with a polystyrene cup of black coffee in my left hand. My right elbow is slid along the desk, my right hand supporting both the telephone receiver and my head. My back is against the swivel chair, and I am swinging slightly to and fro.

'Who's paying?'

'Well I am, naturally.'

This is ridiculous. I have rung Mother only to let her know, out of politeness and duty, that I won't be around next week, and I am being subjected to the Spanish Inquisition. It's typical. I chuckle.

'What are you laughing at?'

'Nothing.'

'Well, I don't think it's funny that you pay for everything. You know I don't. You know what *I* feel about Alan.'

Yes, and I don't need telling about it again.

'Why doesn't he get a proper job?'

I take a slurp of coffee, but it burns my tongue, so I put the cup down again. Always the trouble if you have it black, but milk adds calories so I never have it.

'Mother, I can't really discuss this now. I'm in the office.'

'When are you going on this jolly?'

'Next week – off on Monday, back Friday. Just a flying visit.'

'A flying visit that's going to cost you money. I don't understand why a man of his age can't get himself a job. What is he? Forty?'

'Forty-one.'

'Forty-one. Exactly. Too old for you anyway. And why is he living with his mother? He shouldn't be living at home – not at forty-one. And he shouldn't be letting you pay for everything.'

'He's got no money, Mum. Actors are always poor, unless they are very lucky.'

'He should have realised by now that he wasn't going to be a success. That's what a proper man would have done. I knew a nice actor when I was working in market research last year who was always out of work, but there he was, in the office with me, earning money, analysing reports. He didn't have a bean. Kenneth – that was his name. Once a week he made himself a great bowl of batter which he kept in the fridge, and he used to cook some of it up every night and live on it. But he was earning a living, you see, and economising, not expecting some unfortunate woman to keep him.'

I try the coffee again. Still too hot.

'And living with his mother! How can you stand it?'

'He's Jewish – he's being a good Jewish boy, Mum.'

'And that's another thing. They'll never accept you. They never do. If it came to marriage they wouldn't want to know. Marrying out. They don't like it.'

Why am I bothering with this pointless call? I've got work to do. The building is stirring, people are coming in – I can see them out of the window down below, walking past the Ariel fountain and in through main reception. And I can see silhouettes in the offices opposite (in a round building you can see across the central well – if you are on the inside). Silhouettes taking off coats, sitting down at desks, lifting telephones.

I slide my arm further down the desk, the phone clamped to my ear, and reach out for the coffee again. The polystyrene cup doesn't feel so hot now, so I cautiously take a sip. Better – quite drinkable.

'Alan's family are all lovely to me. What do you mean, they won't want to know me? They like knowing me, and I like knowing them.'

'Yes, but if it came to marriage—'

'I don't want it to come to marriage. Anyway, Alan's first wife was non-Jewish and no one made a fuss about it.'

'That didn't last long, did it? His mother put paid to that.'

'I love Alan's mother. She's great. She buys me tins of baked beans with pork sausages in them for supper because she knows I like them. Even though she's Kosher. And Alan is a dear. And he's nice to you, as well.'

'Yes, yes, that's true. But he will always put his mother first. You mark my words. And he ought to pay his share.'

'If I was an out-of-work actress and my gentleman friend was in a good job in television, with a salary and regular increases, you would expect *him* to pay for *me*. So why is this different?'

My lady producer enters the office in a whirl of coats and scarves, carrying the regulation polystyrene cup of coffee in her hand, her bag looped over the other arm. She looks at me, and makes an irritated noise through her nose as she throws her coat and scarf onto the pegs on the wall.

She sits down at her desk, eyeing me balefully. I think she is going to be difficult today. I see a little black devil on her shoulder whispering mischief into her ear.

*There was a little girl, and she had a little curl, right in the middle of her forrid; And when she was good she was very very good and when she was bad she was horrid.*

Today is going to be one of her horrid days.

I move the telephone from my ear and say, 'Sorry – won't be a minute,' to her.

'Whenever you're on your own in here you get on the phone, talking to your mother,' she says angrily. She takes a packet of cigarettes from her bag, pushing one out and placing it in her mouth. After scrabbling in the handbag she produces a lighter and starts, crossly, trying to light it.

'Hurry up,' she hisses, through clenched teeth, still holding the cigarette in her mouth and the lighter to the tip.

'You've gone away. Where are you?' quacks the telephone. I put it to my ear again.

'Here – but not for long. I've got to go, Mum. We're busy.'

A cloud of smoke blows over towards me from the lit cigarette. My producer is dropping the lighter back into her bag and turning her wrist over, looking at her watch.'

'We can *never* talk. It's not the same thing anyway. It's a matter of principle. The man pays. He should get a job. In a nice office, nine to five.'

'He wants to act, Mum. Or write. Goodbye, I'm going now. Don't forget I'm away next week.'

'So long as you know that this is very unsatisfactory . . .'

I replace the receiver on the cradle.

'Sorry, I had to tell Mum I am going away next week,' I say, getting up and putting my empty cup in the waste-paper basket.

'Oh, so you are,' says the lady producer. 'With Alistair.'

'Alan,' I say, going back to my desk.

'Whoever,' she says impatiently.

'What's up, then?' I ask her. 'You seem a little fretty.'

She draws deeply on the cigarette, puffing the smoke up

into her hair, where there is a yellow nicotine streak in the grey. Then she puts it in the ashtray in front of her, where it glows sulkily, smoking fiendishly. She drains her coffee.

'What's up is, we are going to be borrowed by Children's Department. Just like that. Without a by-your-leave. We will be doing a co-production with dreadful Duncan Barrow.'

'You don't like Duncan Barrow.'

'Precisely,' she says, taking off her glasses and polishing the lenses with her handkerchief.

'We're doing a remake of *Swallows and Amazons*, on a shared budget, and don't look like that because I got it from the horse's mouth last night. The horse herself rang me at home.'

I walk over to her desk and take her empty cup away.

'Mind you,' she says, looking up at me short-sightedly, 'it might be good news for you.'

'In what way?'

'They might upgrade you to assistant director on extra money.'

I drop the cup into the bin, stunned.

'Really?'

'Well, the horse asked me last night whether I thought you would be up to it.' She replaces her glasses and darts me a wicked look.

'So of course I said you would be splendid.'

Oh no, she didn't. I know that expression.

'One thing, though. If we do this, please don't fall in love with the beastly Duncan Barrow,' she says, looking straight at me.

'Why would I?'

'You might. But don't. Because he will ruin your life.'
Now *she's* starting – and she's not the mothering type.
It must be me.

# The Wedding Day (1966)

Last Friday was my wedding day. It was awful.

I am sitting in the marital home. This is a studio flat off
Kensington Church Street, boasting twin beds and a dining
table with two chairs, a kitchenette and a bathroom. And a television set. All it has to recommend it is the smart address.
And what my husband wanted was a smart address. The rental
reflects this.

I daresay I am the only bride who has ever travelled to her
reception on the tube, with her husband's daughter by his first
marriage in tow. In tears. Not me, her.

She is sixteen. She really knows how to stir things up. So
she did.

The reception was in a French restaurant near Leicester
Square. The food was lovely and Mother had ordered a beautiful cake from a bakery in Blackheath. All that was good.

But the sixteen-year-old was a problem. Weeping and wailing, saying she never believed her father would do this (marry
me and leave her mother). Aunts Mollie and Norah, and
my mother, were nonplussed. They had never experienced

anything like it before. All being sheltered – or, as my mother puts it, 'gently brought up'.

I get up from the dining chair I am sitting on and wander into the kitchenette, looking for the cardboard box in which repose the ruins of the wedding cake.

I find it and lift it from the shelf, putting it on the narrow working surface. Rummaging in the drawer beneath produces a bread knife, with which I hack off a large slice, making sure I get plenty of marzipan, icing and the little sugar roses that went round the edge. The plaster bride and groom are already lying in the bottom of the box. I hope this is not symbolic.

I switch the kettle on and unhook a mug from the row hanging below the cupboards. I throw in a teabag, find a plate for the slice of cake, pour scalding water over the teabag, drag some milk from inside the door of the extremely small fridge and slop it into the mug. Now I can walk back to my dining chair, and eat my cake and slurp my tea in peace.

And as I do it the telephone rings. I put the tea and the cake on the table and go out into the lobby (which is a little smaller than the fridge) to answer it. I know who it will be before I lift the receiver to my ear.

'Well – I hope you enjoyed your day. I certainly didn't.'

Mummy. On the warpath – or maybe in the jungle protecting her tiger cub would be a better analogy?

'What do you mean?'

'You know what I mean,' she crackles. 'That terrible daughter completely ruined it for you. Didn't she? What was he doing, letting her take over like that?'

'Oh Mum – you can't blame him.'

'I can and I do. What did you have to go and marry him

for? You should have known better. You're not a child. You're thirty. And he's fifty. It's all wrong.'

'I love him.' (I think. I hope.)

'Yes – well, I don't. And neither does your father. Your father thinks he's a bag of wind.'

Oh come now. He's an artist. A drama television producer. Of course, she wouldn't understand.

'You're just not used to people like him.'

'I wouldn't want to get used to them.'

If I pull the telephone wire out to its full extent I think I can just sit down at that chair and get at my tea and cake. Cautiously I manoeuvre myself and the receiver in that direction.

'Where've you gone?'

'Just moving into the sitting room, so I can get at my tea, Mum.'

'And that's another thing. Expecting you to live in a place like that. It's just a box – where's the storage space?'

'Mummy, don't start being unreasonably critical . . .'

'I'm not being. I'm right. No question.'

I chew at a piece of cake I have broken off.

'You are not going to help my marriage to flourish if you take this attitude,' I say.

'What are you eating?'

'Bit of the cake. It's lovely.'

'Wasted. All wasted. People felt very uncomfortable at that reception.'

'By "people" I imagine you mean Mollie and Norah?'

'And me. And your father. But I've said to him, "She's made up her mind, we'll just have to put up with it and support her."'

'So why aren't you, then?' I drink some of my tea. This is going to go on and on.

'We shall expect him to put you first. So far, he's failed the test. Giving way to that terrible daughter like that. No one was looking at you. They were all looking at her. What she wanted of course. Why didn't he stop her?'

I think I am probably going to explode now. I bang down the mug. She must know this is giving me stress, dividing my loyalties.

'If it's any comfort he doesn't like you any more than you like him,' I say, loudly.

'Keep your voice down.'

'I'll say what I like as loudly as I like in my own home.'

'Home! I wouldn't call it that.'

'He calls you the "Witch of the South Coast".'

'He doesn't! Why?'

'Ask yourself that question.'

'If you are going to be like this, then I haven't got a daughter. I just have to tell myself I don't have a daughter at all any more.'

Here we go again.

'Don't be silly. I can love you as well as him. The fact that *you* don't like each other needn't come into it.'

There is the sound of a key in the front door. My husband is home.

'Got to go now, Mum. Duncan's back.'

I take the telephone receiver back into the hall to replace it in the cradle, hearing my mother's voice crackling, 'You can still talk to me, can't you?'

I encounter my husband in the hall, receiver in hand, as I put it down.

'Talking to the Witch of the South Coast again, are we?' he asks, thinly. 'Terrible woman. The sooner you realise that the better.'

I wouldn't know. She's my mother. She and I will go on talking to the end.

# THE END STORY

THE END STORY

# I Know Who's Responsible (2005)

Last Friday was my wedding day. My second wedding day. The Triumph of Hope over Experience – forty years later. It was lovely.

Mother came, in a wheelchair. One hundred and two and half-blind. All the same, she had to be there. She couldn't see my husband, of course. But she liked his voice.

Afterwards, she patted my hand and said, 'I think that's a very nice man, dear.' I got it right at last it would seem.

Today I am visiting her in the care home. She is settling down – or is she becoming institutionalised?

We sit in the music room, Mother squashed up on a two-seater sofa with her friend Vi, holding a mug of tea against her chest. I perch on the window-ledge next to a vase of daffodils so that I am close to her good ear.

She is wearing a summer top with a pair of winter trousers – someone else's as they are too big for her. Outside the garden looks spring-like. Things are budding – starting life. Inside, the few residents in the music room are wilting. Waves of warm air steam through the vents in the heating unit below the window-ledge.

My mother stretches her arm out, feeling shakily for the

table. Then she wobbles her mug of tea onto the edge. It looks precarious. I push it on further with my finger.

'I don't have no milk in my tea,' Vi tells me, showing me the contents of her mug. 'I don't have no milk and no sugar.' She drinks deeply.

The tea-trolley rolls through, back from its rounds, with a cheerful Vietnamese girl in a blue uniform doing the steering.

'Hi,' calls my mother. 'We could do with some tea here.'

'You had some, Muriel,' sings the carer. 'You want more?'

'Mum, we've had tea. Look. There's yours, in front of you,' I say, smiling at the blue uniform.

'There's my what?' Mother peers ahead, seeing little.

'It's OK, Tina,' I say. 'Take no notice.'

'What do you mean, "Take no notice"? I heard that.' Mother is aggrieved.

Tina starts wheeling the trolley past us on its way to the kitchen.

'By the way, Tina, Mum's wearing someone else's trousers today. Can you sort her out later?' I sound apologetic. They are short-staffed.

Tina beams. 'OK,' she says, and trundles past us.

I put my mother's mug of tea in her hand, and curl her fingers round the handle.

'There's your tea. And you've got a half-eaten biscuit on the table.'

'Got a what?'

I put the biscuit into her other hand.

'A biscuit. Now finish it. Mind the crumbs.'

There is a burst of nursery-rhyme music from CBeebies, as the small television set chunters to itself in the corner of the room.

'There's a move afoot to send me away from here,' says my mother through her biscuit. 'To be a schoolteacher.'

'Don't be ridiculous, Mother.'

'I can't be a schoolteacher. I can't see. I can't hear.'

'I look after her,' says Vi, looking down on Mother indulgently. 'I keep my eye on her. She sleeps most of the time.'

'Mother, of course you aren't going to have to be a school-teacher.'

'What's more, I know who's responsible.' Mother nods in the direction of another resident, slumped in a wheelchair. 'That man over there,' she says.

The resident wakes with a start, then goes back to sleep.

'I wish I could die,' says Mother fretfully.

'They haven't got your place ready yet,' I say. 'You're so fussy, they're having to go round dusting everything.'

My mother laughs.

'Tell me about the jellied eel stall,' I say. 'What do jellied eels smell like?'

'Awful,' she says.

'And right outside your bedroom window, too,' I say.

'What was?'

# I Haven't Had Any Dinner (2005)

Mother is in her own room this afternoon. Alone, in her dressing-gown, her tiny white shoulder protruding from a skimpy flowered nightie. A pair of brocade slippers in electric blue with a Velcro fastening complete the outfit. Her bare feet are jammed into these, showing inflamed skin round her ankles, and there are some worrying purple patches on her lower legs. She seems OK. Maybe I should mention the legs to the manager when I go out?

I am sitting in a wheelchair which has been left in the room. I wheel myself up close to her so that she can hear me.

'What's been happening, then?' I ask.

She leans forward in the armchair, dislodging a fluffy cushion with the word 'CUDDLES' embroidered on it. Put there for her comfort by someone – origin unknown. Certainly it's not hers.

'Well,' she begins. 'That woman who used to live opposite. What was her name?'

'Kitty?'

'What?'

'KITTY.'

'Yes. Kitty. She's been to prison.'

'Been to prison! Don't be daft – of course she hasn't been to prison.'

'Shhh! Keep your voice down. She's a very proud woman.'

'Mother! What did she go to prison *for*?'

'Mmmm?'

'I said, what did she go to prison for?'

'Something to do with men.'

She leans back in the chair again, encountering the 'CUDDLES' cushion which is now sticking into the small of her back.

'What's this thing?' She struggles to remove it.

'Just a silly cushion.' I reposition it so that it is supporting her slightly. 'How's that?'

'How's what?'

'Never mind. Anyway, they don't send 95-year-old ladies to prison. Not 95-year-old ladies with a catheter and confined to a wheelchair.'

'There's nothing wrong with her. Kitty? She's perfectly all right. I've seen her walking about.'

'I'm telling you, she's confined to a wheelchair and she's in very poor nick.'

Mother fidgets crossly.

'Anyway, that's my news. Take it or leave it as you please.'

I look round the room. They have given her new curtains in a creamy polyester with black swirls.

'How do you like your curtains?'

'Awful,' is the reply.

Opposite the window her bed looks like a bring-and-buy sale. I can see two different-coloured blankets layered under a crocheted, multicoloured rug, with a cream cellular blanket on top. She has four pillows, each with a different patterned cover. Lying on the pillows are a small stuffed cat and a miniature stuffed teddy-bear wearing slippers and a bathrobe.

'Why aren't you dressed?' I ask.

'I don't put any clothes on because it's too much bother. Keep a nightie on and a dressing-gown. That's all. They don't seem to mind. Anyway, they forget me.'

'What do you mean, they forget you?'

'What do I what?'

'They forget you. What do you mean?'

'Well, I haven't had any dinner.'

'But it's only four o'clock.'

'I mean middle-day dinner.'

'Well, if they don't feed you then you will die. And you want to die, don't you?'

'Yes. But when it comes to it, you don't like it.'

There is a swishing of feet along the corridor outside and a clattering sound.

'Knock, knock,' calls a voice.

Mother's door is wedged open. All the doors are always open. It is a rule.

A face appears round the door. 'Who wants a cuppa?'

Dee, Mother's chief carer, enters, holding two mugs. 'Where's a good place to put these?'

We pull the little invalid's table round between us and she puts the mugs down.

'Mum says you haven't fed her today,' I say jokingly. But I need to know.

Dee crouches down by Mother's chair.

'You what?' she says. 'You naughty old granny. You had shepherd's pie and greens. And you had a second helping. Don't you remember?'

'Had what?' says Mother.

'Shepherd's pie. You had two helpings.'

'Did I? I've forgotten.'

'You're a silly old granny,' says Dee fondly. She pats my mother's hand, scrambles to her feet, and whisks through the door again, before returning with two paper napkins wrapped round something.

'Joe's made ginger cake. Who wants some?'

She dumps the little parcels on the table.

'Not for me, Dee,' I say. But she has gone.

Mother picks at the cake, dropping crumbs down her nightie.

'Listen! Listen!' she says.

'What?'

'I've forgotten.'

She chews thoughtfully and stretches out for the mug of tea, which I move into her grasp.

'I'm trying to tell you something,' she goes on, holding the mug at a dangerous angle. 'I'm trying to tell you what happened to me between Sunday and I don't know when it was. I don't know what I was doing up there anyway, but I got in with these people who were – who were trying to get onto the list. And I was treated like a princess for a day, and I thought, "This is lovely" but of course it wasn't.'

I take the mug away from her and put it back on the table.

'Who were these people?'

'I'm trying to tell you. It wasn't lovely because I wasn't any good.'

'Not any good at what?'

'Oh, listen, do. All these people wanted to get onto the list and somehow I got in with these people who were hoping to be – oh dear, I am so stupid. Hoping to be . . . Well, I was interviewed and they said no. It was all really a mistake on their part. They have apologised. There was one man who was terribly lenient and wanted to keep me. But I didn't want to be kept anyway. Although I thought, "This is the life."'

She reaches out for the mug again and puts trembling lips to it, before replacing it on the edge of the table. As usual I push it on further. We drink our tea in silence for a while, Mother fumbling for the cake, eating some and dropping the rest.

'Mum. You remember Paul?'

'Who?'

'PAUL.'

'Yes. Paul. I heard.'

'He's got a new lady-friend.'

'Well, the girls don't seem to settle down.'

'What girls?'

'Did you say it was sad?'

'No. I said, "What girls?"'

'Mmmmmm.'

'You didn't hear that, did you?'

'Write it down.'

'You can't read. You can't see.'

'No. But you never know. I hear all about it, you see. And I hope you're not in it.'

'In what?'

'*Don't shout.*'

'We found a way of talking to each other *without* shouting once. What was it?'

'Can't remember.'

'Neither can I.'

Mother laughs, choking on the cake crumbs.

# Who Was That Chap I Married? (2006)

They have moved the furniture round in Mother's room today. Or, to be accurate, they did it yesterday. Mother is more confused than usual, and thinks they have put her in another room altogether. She has one elbow on the arm of her chair, and her head in her hand – her usual position for worrying.

As I sit down in the visitors' chair and pull it up closer to her, she says, 'The last time you came here, there was an accident – and I thought, "There you are – Doodie's in that."'

She takes her hand away from her face and looks at me, her forehead a rambler's map of tracks.

Before I can answer, big Maggie enters, kicking the door open wider with her foot, carrying Mother's supper on a tray.

'Here we go, Muriel,' she says, banging it down on the little table, and pushing it up towards her. 'A nice ham sandwich.'

'Hi, Maggie,' I smile. 'What's going on? With the room?'

Maggie turns round, looking at the new arrangements.

'What do you think? Better, isn't it?' she says, pleased with herself.

'Here! Where's the salt?' says Mother.

'Behind the curtains where you hide it,' says Maggie, twitching them aside, rescuing the salt cellar from the window-ledge and putting it on Mother's tray.

'Better in what way?' I ask.

'Oh, she had all these wires trailing. Absolute death-trap,' says Maggie. 'Look, we've tidied them up *here*' – she lifts up the valance of the bed, showing a mare's nest of plugs and flexes attached to a red plastic drum – 'and we put the bed round this way so that she can get to the loo easier. It's much better.'

'Well, I can see the point,' I say. 'But it's bothering her.'

'She'll get used to it,' says Maggie. She bends over Mother's stooped figure. 'Won't you, darling?' she says loudly. 'See you later.' And she is gone, half-closing the door behind her.

I get up and go to adjust the curtains. I see a whiskered face at the window. Two greengage eyes regard me steadily from outside.

'The cat wants to come in,' I say, over my shoulder.

'Well, let him in – but I'm not speaking to him,' says Mother.

I open the window and Orlando shoots through, bolting over the ledge and down onto the floor. He is gone in a marmalade streak.

'He doesn't want to speak to you either.'

'He scratched me last week and I hit him,' she says.

I turn from the window and see she has not touched her sandwich, or her mug of tea.

'No wonder he doesn't want a cosy chat, then. Why aren't you eating your supper?'

The curtain billows in the wind.

'I'm not eating it because it's yours.'

'No, it's not. I don't need it. I shall have supper at home.'

'Will you get a taxi back, or stay the night?'

'I'm not staying the night. I've got a home and a husband.'

I shut the window and latch it, tidying the curtains so that they meet neatly.

Mother looks up from her tray.

'Well, he can look after himself for one night.'

I go back to the visitor's chair, and sit next to her.

'He looked dreadful when he came here to tell me about your accident.'

'What accident?'

Mother picks at her sandwich.

'It was all in the papers for about three days.'

'I haven't had an accident.'

'In France – you were in hospital in France. I was so worried.'

'It didn't happen. I haven't had an accident.'

'I knew you had. You must be more careful.'

It is best not to pursue this sort of conversation. Best to change the subject.

Mother is eating her sandwich, munching slowly, her eyes focused on the middle distance.

'How's the sandwich?'

'It tastes funny.'

'How, funny?'

'It doesn't taste of fish.'

'Why would it? It's a ham sandwich.'

'A what?'

'A HAM SANDWICH.'

'All right. Keep your voice down. Don't keep on saying it. Goodness knows. It's not baked. It's not cooked. What are you having?'

'We're having goujons of sole.'

'*Two shelves?*'

Mother picks up her mug of tea and carries it to her lips, one hand underneath it. Her underlip trembles as she sips. She puts the mug down again, and pushes the remains of the sand-wich about with her finger.

'Did I tell you that I'd moved? I had one night in this room, but the young man was terribly angry because he thought it was his place.'

'Mother,' I say. 'You're confused.'

'Well, I know that. Of course I am.'

'It's the same room, Mum. They've just moved the furni-ture round a bit.'

'I came in first thing in the morning, as is my wont. I said, "I'm going up to my little hovel up there." They're not going to let it, are they?'

She pushes at her plate of half-finished sandwich.

'I don't want this. It's yours.'

'I don't want it, Mum.'

'I know, but in the morning you will and you won't get much breakfast here. We'll have to decide if we're going home or staying the night here.'

'I'm not staying!'

'Brave girl. John would have waited till the morning. Our John.'

It's change-the-subject time again. I get up and take the tray away from her, putting it on the chest of drawers. Then I go back to the armchair next to her and take one of her hands.

'Do you remember a girl here?' she asks me.

'What girl?'

'She's cropped up again.'

'Cropped up again what?'

'Well, you and I, we wanted – um, we both, er—'

'Either tell me the story or shut up.'

'Well, that's it, isn't it?'

'Come on. Get on with it, or don't bother.' I look at my watch. Time is getting on. I will give her another five minutes.

'She's cropped up again and she's had £2,000 and she's much to the fore and wants to do everything. And she says I owe her £50.'

'Mum, you don't owe anybody anything.'

'You remember. That girl. She came from Wales and I thought, "Why doesn't she get married and live in Wales?" Anyway, I didn't ask her why she didn't. She's cropped up again. We've had such a silly weekend. This girl, she was mad keen to marry me. I don't know why, but she was. She came with another girl. That girl I owed money to. I thought perhaps she is thinking she might get £50 as well. But I don't think she was that sort of girl.'

'I keep telling you – you don't owe anybody anything.'

'No. That chap said I didn't.'

'What chap?'

'You know. That chap I married. What was his name?'

'Do you mean my father?'

'Yes. That's right. What was he called?'

'Laurence.'

'Well, I don't owe anybody now. Not now I've paid this girl £50.'

'Paid someone £50? When was this?' I let go of her hand.

I feel anxious now. Mother, who used to be so careful with money, might have done anything. She is not as she was. She is another mother.

'When? Oh this was all before you came on the scene.'

Someone is ringing their bell. There are hurrying footsteps down the corridor outside.

Mother, who cannot hear any of it, leans back in her chair, and closes her eyes.

Our conversation is over. For today.

# Kitty's Getting Married (2007)

Mother's room faces north because that is what she prefers. She refused offers of south-facing rooms from the outset. No one else understands this except me, as no one else understands how averse she is to the sun. Especially the sun through glass.

Today the old farmhouse building that is the care home stands in fields shimmering with heat, under a pitiless sky. I wait at the front door to be let in and I can feel the warmth radiating from the plate glass in the front door. A bee buzzes. A light aircraft meanders overhead. I see residents drowsing in their chairs at the open windows. Why aren't they out of doors, in the garden?

A diminutive figure in a blue uniform brandishing an enormous bunch of keys appears, advancing on the door. It is Billie, her oval face shining with pleasure.

'Hello. Hello, Judit,' she says as she opens the door. 'Mother in her room.'

'How is she in this hot weather?' I ask, as I walk past her into the hall.

'She complaining a lot,' laughs Billie. But she always laughs.

I make my way down the corridor, hoping not to find Mother pallid and collapsed. As I reach her door, which bears the photograph of a white kitten with the word 'MURIEL' below it, I catch sight of her cream pleated skirt, her white legs and brilliant blue Velcro slippers and the edge of her armchair in front of the window. Not lying moaning on the bed then. A good sign.

She looks up as I go in.

'They take your dressing-gowns to wash them,' she complains. 'And when you get them back they are all different.'

'That's bad,' I say, wondering what this is about. I sit on the end of the bed, moving her stuffed kitten to make room.

'How much do you think I ought to pay them to give me a bath?'

'You don't pay them. It's all free. You're in a care home. You're not allowed to pay them.'

Mother looks at me, screwing up her eyes, making sure it is me. It is cool and dim in here and I am relieved she is not being cooked like a greenhouse tomato. Through the open door I can see one of the rooms opposite, consumed by sunlight, like a small furnace.

'How do you like the weather?'

'Terrible,' she replies.

'But you're all right in here,' I say.

Through her open window, I can see the newly built patio. It took six months to do, caused uproar and confusion while they were doing it, and lies there, baking, and empty. Surely they could take people outside – put up a little gazebo or something?

'You should all be outside,' I say. 'In the garden, under the trees. Or under sunshades on the patio.'

'Kitty's outside,' she says.

'No, she's not. No one's outside.'

'Be that as it may. She's getting married, you know.'

She feels for the water jug on the small table in front of her. I get up from the bed, find a glass on the window-ledge and fill it, putting it down before her. The jug is nearly empty. That will be the next thing. Judy the Water-Carrier.

'Nonsense. Of course she's not getting married.'

'He's in the army. An officer.'

'Well, if he's still in the army he has to be much younger than her.'

'He's sixty, I think.'

'Mother! Do you know how old Kitty is?'

'About your age, isn't she?'

'And how old am I?' I sit down on the edge of the bed again.

'Well, er . . .'

'I'm seventy-one, Mother. Are you telling me Kitty is only seventy-one?'

'Well, no – obviously that would be ridiculous.'

'She's ninety-four. She's in a wheelchair with a catheter in her leg. She's not getting married.'

'She always liked her men young.'

Mother grasps her glass of water in both hands and gulps.

The heat vibrates outside. No wind, no shade. A small striped fly hovers between the open window and the frame. It looks like a wasp, but it is tiny. They have a name, those little flies, but I have forgotten what it is.

'Well, never mind,' I say to Mother, taking the glass from her fingers and putting it on the table. 'How's your other friend?'

'Which other friend?'

'The new little friend you told me about.'

'Oh, that little one? I was expecting her today, but I think she doesn't come in case she bores me. She thinks if she comes too often she will bore me and I think so too. How is your husband's garden?'

'It's not much yet. We're going to get a gardener in.'

'Going to get a child in?'

'NO. A GARDENER!'

'Keep your voice down. Don't shout. That's what it sounds like to me. I'm very cross with them, mucking up my ear. I can't hear properly and I don't know what they're doing. I can't see properly now my eyes have got very bad. There is nothing they can do. I saw an optician man today and he said, "Oh you have got a little bit of sight," and I said, "I know, but it's no good for reading." I feel it's a burden on you to have to do everything all the time.'

She reaches out and pats my hand.

'Excuse me. Excuse me, ladies!'

The door is being pushed open and potty Edna is entering. Very businesslike and purposeful.

'Come in, Edna,' says Mother.

'No, I won't stay. I can see you are busy,' says Edna. She walks to the window and stands looking out of it, hands clasped behind her back.

'Just checking,' she says. 'Checking to make sure no one's trapped out there.'

She looks right and left, stands on tiptoe briefly, then turns to us smiling.

'No. Everything's OK.' She marches across the room to the door.

'Goodbye, ladies,' she says as she goes.

Mother and I laugh.

'She's quite dotty, that one,' says Mother.

She pulls a tissue out of the box on the chest of drawers, and wipes her brow and her hands.

'That girl's come back. You know. The one you said wasn't. Well, she is. I like to watch these girls. They're – oh, what is the word I want?'

She screws up the tissue into a ball and hands it to me.

'Put that in the bin for me, will you?'

I get up, find the bin, and drop the tissue into it. Then I move over to her.

'Mum. I'm going to take an MA. I shall have a degree and a mortarboard,' I say loudly.

She looks up at me, surprised.

'You're going to take a degree with the Water Board?'

'No – degree, with a MORTARBOARD.'

'My clever daughter,' she says.

She picks up the water jug, weighing it in her hands, and peers into it.

'I think this is empty. Will you fill it for me before you go? They never do it.'

They fill it twice a day. But she likes to keep me busy. Judy the Water-Carrier it is, then.


# I Didn't Know What I Was Doing (2008)


There are more people in the music room than usual. Space is at a premium since the management have decided to get the residents' lounge redecorated. The music room used to be just that. Somewhere you went to be quiet and listen to music. But last year the management plonked a television set in here – where it is squawking to itself. So it isn't a quiet place any more.

Outside in the narrow corridor a workman is cheerfully slapping paste on paper stretched on a board between two trestles, singing lustily.

Inside, people battle for places to sit. This morning we have Pauline, seated upright, expressionless; a new resident called Evelyn who is reading a magazine with a leg draped over the arm of her chair, her ballet-slippered foot dangling; and dotty Edna. Edna is waving a pretend pistol and going 'Bang, bang' as people pass. There are others there I don't recognise, mostly staring at the walls.

One lady in a wheelchair appears to be watching the small, babbling television set in the middle of the room. There is a strong smell of mince and onions in the air. That is because it is Monday.

Mother and Vi are squeezed together on a two-seater arrangement by the window. The little coffee table in front of them has the remains of elevenses on it – biscuit crumbs and two mugs with cold coffee dregs in the bottom.

'Hi, Mum,' I say. 'Tell me about everything.'

'I wish I could.'

'Go on. Try. What's been going on?'

'Well—' She pauses, brushing imaginary crumbs from her skirt. She doesn't notice the coffee-stains on her blouse. Vi shifts uncomfortably.

'Nice to see you, dear,' says Vi.

'Nice to see *you*, Vi. How are you?'

'Fed up. I haven't had no visitors this week.'

Mother resumes her narrative.

'Well, people who are supposed to be dead, aren't dead.'

'Do you mean Kitty?'

'Yes. So am I.'

'Kitty died six weeks ago, Mother.'

'Bang, bang,' calls Edna. 'You're dead!'

'Bang, bang,' I reply. 'Got you.'

'Kitty? I've seen her and she's perfectly well.'

'Don't be silly. She's dead.'

'Be that as it may.'

Something is wrong with my mother's appearance. She looks drawn, her face seems to have caved in. I look at her hard.

'Open your mouth, Mum.'

She obliges.

'Where are your teeth? What's happened to them?'

'Those front teeth – when you're in a deep sleep you might not feel them being removed.'

'You don't think someone's pinched them?'

'It's a possibility.'

'But where are they? And where is your hearing aid?'

'Don't look for him. He's not here.'

'BANG, BANG, BANG.'

'No, no, no – you don't love me any more,' sings the decorator in the corridor.

CEEBEEBEECEE! carols the television.

'Oh well,' I say, patting Mother's hand. 'Never mind.'

'I do mind. I mind terribly about my teeth.'

'She didn't have them in yesterday,' offers Vi. 'She hasn't had them all week.'

'You must be more careful with them. We can't go on replacing them. That's £600-worth gone.'

'Sixty pounds? Oh, how dreadful!'

'Not sixty. SIX HUNDRED POUNDS.'

'Oh my dear. Well, I often take them out in the night, but I don't often lose them. I take them out at night and put them back in the morning. Do I look awful?'

'Put it this way. Not awful – but it's not a good look.'

Mother glances around the room and her sightless gaze settles on Pauline. She retains a fuzzy peripheral vision, although macular degeneration has claimed most of her eyesight.

'Can you get rid of that lady on the sofa?' she says to me loudly. 'She's been there since coffee-time.'

'Mother, don't be rude. That's Pauline. She's entitled to be here.'

'The only way you could get rid of her is to say, "Do you mind moving?"'

I decide it is better to change the subject. A gleam of sunshine appears, dappling the carpet.

'Did you sit outside in the sun yesterday?'

'Yes. Who was it I sat with?'

'I took her round the garden,' says Vi.

'You were with Vi, Mum.'

'No, I wasn't with Vi. I didn't go with Vi.'

Vi shrugs.

'Can't you get rid of her? That woman over there. She's one of those that sits.'

'It's my birthday on Saturday, Mum. What are you going to give me?' I say, hoping to distract her attention.

'Why is it your birthday on Saturday?'

'Because you happened to give birth to me seventy-two years ago on Saturday.'

'Did I? I didn't know what I was doing.'

She smiles ruefully and takes my hands in hers, patting them and smoothing them.

'Nice little hands,' she says. Then, 'When you go, will you take that woman with you? Say, "Wouldn't you like to come with me?" Of course, then you'd be saddled with her, though, wouldn't you?'

'It's nearly dinnertime,' says Vi. 'Monday mince.'

'BANG BANG,' says Edna.

'Guess what, Mum?' I say. 'Esther Rantzen is standing for parliament!'

'Who's she?'

'You know – had a lot of front teeth.'

'Didn't have any front teeth?'

'That's not what I said.'

'I don't know where my teeth are. I think the girls pinch them.'

'Are we going to get you some new ones? Are we going to spend another £600?'

'Oh yes, because I've just found a nice young man here. I've taken a fancy to him. His name is Davie. He's new.'

'Davie's been here for ages, Mum.'

'Oh, he's lovely. Do I look awful without my teeth?'

The handsome Davie appears with a wheelchair to take Mother in to lunch, his face beaming with goodwill and his smile broad.

'Mother's in love with you, Davie,' I say.

He helps Mother into her chair, laughing his deep laugh.

'Bye, Mum,' I say, giving her a kiss.

'I don't know what to do about that woman. Will you take her with you when you go?'

She moves off happily, leaving me to wonder where another £600 is coming from.

It's no good, I must Take Things Further.

Along the corridor is the door saying MANAGER in large

letters. As a rule this office is empty, but this time, there she is, sitting at her desk.

I knock on the glass panel and put my head round into her space.

'So – can *you* solve the mystery of Mother's missing dentures, then?' I ask.

'Oh, Judy, we've looked everywhere,' she says, getting up and coming towards me.

'We've had the place upside down and inside out. We've checked everyone's rooms, all the bins . . .'

'It's not good enough, though, is it?' I say.

'Well, she could have done anything with them – that's the problem.' She leans conversationally on the door jamb.

'But it has happened once before, Carol, and it's another expense we can do without.' I know I sound apologetic. Why do I always feel I'm bothering them?

I should be firmer with her. This is serious. But it isn't easy for the carers here. Most of the residents are wanderers, picking things up like children, putting them down, losing them, taking them away, tottering off with them. How can they mount a guard on them all, twenty-four seven? Can't be done.

'We think she wrapped them in a tissue and left them on her chest of drawers, Judy.'

'So why aren't they still on the chest of drawers, then?'

Carol's telephone is ringing – but she ignores it.

'She probably thought it was just a little bundle of used tissues and threw it all in the bin.'

Yes. That is just what she would have done. Whoever emptied the bin would never have known they were in there. How can it be their fault?

I try another tack.

'If we buy a new set, can I ask the home to take care of them? Take responsibility for them?'

Carol decides to go to her desk to answer the insistent telephone. She says over her shoulder, 'Yes. You can. But that would mean we would have to remove them from her mouth every evening. And she might resist that. Probably would. And we can't do it forcibly. It could be difficult. She gets quite aggressive sometimes.'

She reaches the telephone and picks it up.

'Hello? Sunny Lodge. Oh, yes, we were expecting to hear from you.'

She waves at me with her free hand, and points at the mouthpiece, nodding her head, indicating that this is an important call.

Weakly I give in. Maybe there is some insurance cover somewhere we can use?

I move away. Leave it. It's hopeless.

How long is all this going on?

# The Queen Is Visiting (2007)

The care home is at the end of a rough track – no room for two cars to pass unless one driver obligingly moves over into the ditch. Luckily it is not much frequented. It's certainly quiet here. You can hear the birds singing this morning as I park up and negotiate the uneven path to the front door.

Sunny today. It would be hot if it weren't for the wind, which is coming from the east and gusting strongly out in the open here at the top of the hill. I press both front-door bells to make sure someone hears – they're often busy in distant rooms dealing with people who need nursing – as I would prefer to get inside quickly before this wind penetrates to my vital organs.

A smiling face above a blue uniform appears and a hand holding the usual bunch of keys unlocks the door for me.

'Mother OK,' Tina beams. 'She in the music room. How you? You OK?'

I say that I am and pass her, going down the passageway and squeezing through the bottleneck between the residents' lounge and the bathrooms until I am opposite the open door to the music room.

Mother is in her favourite armchair by the window next to her friend Vi. She smiles broadly and puts sparrow-like hands out to me as I approach.

'Here's my daughter!' She turns to Vi. 'Vi, do you know my daughter? Let me introduce you.'

'Oh, Mum, Vi and I are old friends, aren't we, Vi?'

'I haven't had no visitors today,' mourns Vi. Then she adds, 'Nice to see you, dear.'

'So,' I say to Mum, as I settle myself on the window-ledge, there being no available vacant chair, 'What's been happening?' The sun is very hot on the back of my head here, so the position is not ideal.

Mother is bright and positive and hearing me well. She is properly dressed and her hair has been done.

'Tomorrow the Queen's coming to visit me. The problem is, what am I going to wear?'

'I wouldn't worry too much. The Queen's not particularly dressy.'

'No – you're right.'

'She ought to go to the loo,' interrupts Vi, waving an arm towards Mother. 'She's been on about it all afternoon.'

'Do you want the loo, Mother?'

'What? The loo? No. The Queen's been to see lots of people here, you know.'

*Row, row, row your boat, gently down the stream*, chortles the television.

'What's that noise?'

'Only the television.'

Vi is staring vacantly at the screen.

'Turn it off,' says Mum.

'Vi's watching it, aren't you, Vi?'

Vi mumbles and continues staring.

'So the Queen's been here before, has she?' I say to Mother. 'Comes often, does she?'

'Yes. You see the Queen and then you go to the old people's wotsit. Wednesday is her day for visiting, so that's why she's coming tomorrow.'

'But tomorrow's Tuesday.'

'No, it's not. It's Wednesday'

'No, Mum, it's Tuesday. Today is Monday.'

'It's WEDNESDAY.' Mother's voice is rising. She pauses for breath. 'But you can make it Tuesday if you like.' She pats my hand and I see her nails are so long they are bending at the ends.

'Your nails need filing, Mum,' I say.

'My nails what?'

'You've got Struwwelpeter nails. They need filing.'

'I thought they might. I can't see them, you know.'

There is a clattering noise at the door and two carers in their blue uniforms move through the room wheeling an upright contraption carrying Mother's friend Bertram in his pyjamas. Bertram is kneeling, with his hands attached to the uprights, his pyjama trousers slipping to reveal half his behind. His face is as white as the skin on his bottom.

The carers gently manoeuvre him and his torturous conveyance past the television and the sofas to the door into the narrow corridor outside. Where is he going? Are they taking him for a bath?

Vi moves her legs slightly. 'All right? Can you get through?'

'Who's that?' says Mother, turning sightless eyes towards the door.

'Bertram, Mum.'

'Oh him,' she says dismissively.

But I wonder what can have happened to Bertram since I saw him last. He has gone downhill in a big way surely? I get a nail file from my handbag and take one of Mother's small hands into mine.

'Thank you, dear,' she says as I start filing. How can nobody have noticed how neglected my mother's nails have become? I suppose they have too much to do, looking after people like Bertram.

She chatters on as I work.

'Another piece of news is that a man came after dinner to sing to us. So we all sang with him. And he said he recognised a voice when he heard it.'

'What did he mean? Bend your fingers a bit, I can't get at them.' I manage to turn her hand so that I can get at her thumbnail with the file. Her nails are like yellow cardboard.

'He meant that he had decided that my voice was very nice. Ouch.' She flinches as I turn her little finger towards me.

'Sorry. Did he? That's nice. Is it true?'

'No,' says Mother. 'No, it's not true.'

'She ought to go to the loo,' says Vi. She looks at me. 'I been waiting for my sister all day but she hasn't come.'

'Oh dear. That's a shame,' I say to her.

'I haven't seen her all week. Been waiting all week. Still, it's nice to see you, dear.'

'Well, I can't make her into your sister,' says Mother.

'Both doors are open,' says Vi. 'She can go to the loo if she wants. She usually goes herself. I can't take her, you see, in case I fall.'

I put Mother's hands back in her lap and the file into my handbag.

'There. They look much better now.'

Mother peers at them.

'Thank you, dear. Now I really believe that I'm going to see the Queen.'

'Why. Didn't you believe it?'

'No.'

'Did you make it up to amuse yourself?'

'Yes.' She struggles to get to her feet. 'It doesn't matter

about seeing HER. It's seeing YOU that matters, dear,' she says.

'Where are you off to?' I am trying to hold onto her so that she doesn't fall over.

'I must go to the loo,' she says, grasping her stick and beginning a slow progress towards the door and the corridor with the bathrooms.

'I told you,' says Vi.

*CeeBeeBeeCee* . . . gurgles the television.

# They Are All Against My Family (2007)

It is nearly Christmas. A chilly wind whips my scarf from round my neck as I ring the doorbells of the care home and note that they have sellotaped the message 'A Merry Christmas' in multicoloured paper letters on the glass. There is some cottonwool snow glued above it.

After a long wait the door is opened. Blonde, pretty Dee waves me in.

'Sorry – we were dealing with Bertram.' Say no more then, I know he needs a lot of looking after these days.

'Is she in the music room, Dee?'

'To tell you the truth, Judy, I don't know where she is. She's somewhere around,' says Dee, turning to go into the kitchen. Two cardboard Father Christmases swinging from the lintel catch her head as she goes through the door.

'Have you let her escape?' I call after her.

She laughs as I move into the hall and down the corridor, looking for Mother.

Not in the residents' lounge, not in the loo, not in the music room. There is a small, very old and bent resident ahead of me, staggering along, touching the walls for support as she goes. From the back I see that her hair is wild and she is wearing a flowered cotton skirt and a thick roll-necked jumper. She waves a white stick in one hand. I expect I'd better wait until she has got where she is going as there is not room for two of us to pass in the corridor. I stop for a moment.

'There's Mother!' calls one of the carers, coming out of a bathroom, pointing down the corridor.

A blow to the solar plexus. I feel winded. I rarely see my mother walking. She is always sitting with Vi or in her armchair. I hardly recognise the mad little figure ahead of me. But that's her. So frail, so tottery, so crazy-looking. Mummy. The teeny-tiny old woman.

I catch her up, and take her arm.

'What are you doing, wandering down here?' I ask her.

She wobbles, and I grab her round the waist. She looks at me wildly for a moment.

'Oh, it's YOU. Hello, darling. Why have you come?'

Holding her upright, I steer her round the corner to the open door of her own room and propel her across the floor until I can guide her into her armchair by the window. Propping her up with a cushion, I lean her stick against the

side of her chair, within her reach. I then drag the visitors'
chair across the floor so that I am opposite her.

'I've come for a talk,' I say.

But she is angry today, and fretful.

'There's a baby here, and I'm not allowed to see it. That
girl, she got pregnant. And she used this room for – you
know what.'

'Don't be ridiculous.'

'Oh yes, she did. This bed. She certainly did. I don't like
that.'

'Mother. This is your room. Nobody else uses it.'

'They do. There are things left in the bathroom that are
nothing to do with me.'

She looks across at the open door to her small en-suite.

'And I don't like that door open. Close it.'

Obediently I get out of my chair and push the bathroom
door shut, which is hard to do as the bedclothes sticking out
from the bottom of her bed get in the way. You would not
call these rooms spacious.

As I sit down again, she is feeling for her hankie in the
sleeve of her jumper. I pull open the top drawer of her chest
and find a box of tissues. I take a couple out and lay them on
her lap. She dabs at her nose with them.

'You see, I like that door shut.'

'What's your point?'

'Well, I do think people – it's this room and that bed . . .'
She pauses.

I return the box of tissues to the drawer, closing it.

'Don't do that,' she says.

'Don't do what?'

'What?'

'You said, "Don't do that."'

'Don't do what?'

This is a dead-end as far as conversation goes. We often have them.

Big Davie appears, putting his head round the door, smiling his wide smile. In one hand he carries a tiny plastic container, in the bottom of which sits a white tablet; in his other hand is a glass of water. His dark, muscled arm stretches out from the short blue uniform sleeve as he puts the glass down on the chest.

'Here we go, Muriel,' he says. 'Tablet time.'

She takes the little container from him, peers into it, then tips it up into her hand. The tiny tablet lies on her palm, the skin smooth, no longer wrinkled and roughened by housework but shiny, tautened by old age.

Davie gives her the glass and she raises her hand as if she is smacking herself in the mouth. In the movement the tablet goes down her throat and a gulp of water is thrown down after it in a similar fashion. She is obviously used to this routine.

Davie's smile warms the room, and then he is gone.

Mother feels for her paper hanky again in the sleeve of her jumper and wipes her mouth.

'Your hair looks nice today,' I say.

'Does it? I thought it looked dreadful. I don't know what it is, but these girls here, they say to the hairdresser, "Don't make her look nice – make her look horrible." I don't know why they say that.'

She pushes at her hair discontentedly.

'Of course they don't say that. Why would they say that?'

'For the same reason they've got this terrible thing against me because of my ancestors. Saying they were all terrible people. It's not nice. You wouldn't like it.'

'You should be pleased you're interesting enough for people to gossip about you.'

'That woman, she told everyone about our family and I think that's the limit. I said to her, "Well, you'll just have to cut my head off – except you couldn't do it, could you? And you might just do half a job and that would be terrible."'

'Tell me about when your father died. Were you in Shoreditch?'

'We were in Shoreditch. It was awful. I won't ever forget it. He had cancer. And they took him away and he was crying, "Polly, Polly, don't let them take me," and Mother said, "I'll come this afternoon, darling." The bank kept him on and Mother got a big pension.'

I look out of the window across the garden to where I can see the kitchen lit up as it's getting dark. Dee is on a ladder above the cooker, hanging festoons from the light fitting.

'It's getting Christmassy,' I say.

'The trouble is, I can't see my hair.'

'It looks fine.'

'Next Friday? What is today?'

'Monday.'

'Tuesday, Wednesday, Thursday and Friday. I think I'll have a perm. But I'm hoping and praying that every morning when I wake up I won't be there. There won't be any me.'

'That will solve the problem of the hair, then.'

Mother isn't listening.

'My poor mother. She had that terrible thing. Something chopped through her hand and it came right off and it killed her. My father died of cancer in the First World War and my mother had to prepare food. It was very difficult. You had to give up food coupons.'

Someone has pushed their bell. I hear feet hurrying down the corridor outside.

Mother is peering ahead in the gloom, looking at a cake crumb on the carpet.

'What's that there? Oh, that's that pill I take.'

'It isn't. You've taken your pill.'

'I don't know if I've taken it or not.'

'Well, I saw you and you *have* taken it.'

'You saw me and you don't think I've taken it?'

'No. I saw you taking it.'

'Oh.'

'It's going to be cold tonight, Mum.'

'In what way?'

I am too tired to answer this. I think this is the end of our conversation for today. But it will go on again next week – and the week after that. We are locked into an endless duologue, which is going nowhere but which it is impossible to stop. One of us is Scheherazade, although I am not sure which. If one stops, the other will die. Or maybe I feel like this because it's been a long day.

# A Dreadful Day (2008)

Today she is asleep. Leaning up against uncomplaining Vi in the music room. She is wearing a black velours trouser-suit with a sparkly brooch in the shape of a violin on the lapel. This is her Christmas outfit and I wonder why they have chosen to dress her in this in late May.

'I've been looking after her,' says Vi. 'She sleeps most of the time.'

'Hi, Mum,' I say, perching on a coffee table in front of her. 'It's me.'

She opens her eyes unwillingly and squints at me.

'Oh. It's you. I've had a dreadful day. I can't tell you what it's been like.'

*She's* had a dreadful day. What about me? A trip to the gym and a grisly hour's workout, a trip to Sainsbury's to get the weekend shopping and fill the car boot with it, a trip to Marks & Spencer to take two bras back that don't fit – only to find I didn't have my charge-card with me so they couldn't refund the money – a trip to her bank to transfer funds from her reserve account so that I can write a cheque for the replacement of her dentures, and now a trip up here to listen to a lot of rubbish. And I'll have to unload all the shopping when I get back.

'Shall we go upstairs?' she says.

There is no upstairs. This is a single-storey extension to the old farmhouse. 'Upstairs' means her own room, along the corridor and round the right-angled bend at the bottom.

'I'll get you a wheelchair.' She could walk but it would take ten minutes to get to what she calls 'her little hovel'. Time I don't have if I'm to get home and get the dinner on. It's already four o'clock.

I find a user-friendly chair (some of them aren't), unfold it, place it in front of her and engage the brake. Then I help her up, turn her round and encourage her bottom to descend. Eventually she makes it, although there is a worrying wobble before she is safely seated.

I release the brake and off we go. She waves to Vi as she sweeps past.

'See you later, dear,' says Vi.

Mother clutches my handbag on her lap and we make our way cautiously down the narrow corridor with its line of open doors showing occasional glimpses of a bed with a recumbent shape beneath the bedclothes, or a seated figure peering at *Countdown* on a small portable television set. Sometimes this corridor smells of urine and other accidental excretory events, but usually the staff manage to control it. Today it is clean and sweet.

We meet a few inmates attempting to totter up to the residents' lounge. They have to dodge back into their rooms to let us through. (I hope they never have a fire here.)

Finally I have Mother in her own room and settled in her armchair. I sit in the wheelchair with its brake on, as close to her as I can get. I know she is going to tell me about her 'dreadful day' – and she starts.

'I wasn't even consulted,' she begins crossly. 'I didn't know where I was going, but they arranged it. They arranged for these girls to take us. Quite grown-up they were. Students. Oh my God – we went to a place – I don't know – it will come to me. Terrible. Terrible.'

She puts her head in her hands and shakes it. Then looks up again.

'I went in a pushchair and when she got tired this woman – the appendix, as you might say – she wanted to have a ride. So I had to walk. The outcome was I got terribly tired and these girls didn't realise it. Students. I was fed up to the back teeth with them. Then we went to tea with one of them and this girl said she wanted this and that. Chocolate buns. Stuff like that. And I said, "Who's going to pay for it?", as I do.'

My mother was always one for a narrative. Talking was what she did. I am hot, fatigued and thirsty, but Mother is in no mood to stop the flow.

'They had planned it. They thought "Mrs Miles is up to it and the others aren't."'

'HELP ME! HELP ME!' Sudden, loud cries interrupt us.

'The neighbours opposite. I'm afraid they're a bit of a no-no.' Mother is unconcerned.

'Kitty used to live in that room, didn't she?'

'Oh yes, Kitty. She was lovely. But she went to prison, you know.'

Oh God, is she going to start all that again? Better to change the subject.

'Mum, I could murder a cup of tea. I'm so thirsty.'

'So am I, dear. But I want to tell you where we went.'

No escape then.

'These girls, they were sixteen or seventeen and they only had one wheelchair and that girl who lives here – you know the one – she came but she wanted the chair all the time and I was very upset and tired. I wasn't interested in their blooming people. And we had this terrible thing – what's it called? A terrible job. It wasn't a job. It was a terrible make-do thing. Altogether very exhausting.'

'HELP ME! SOMEBODY HELP ME! MUM! BERYL!'

'I'm afraid she's a bit of a ruffian,' says Mother, feeling for her hankie. 'I've got sticky hands. I don't know what I've been eating.' She pulls a tissue out from her sleeve.

'Open the window, will you? It's hot in here.' She wipes her hands as I get up and fumble with the latch on the ventilator. The window sticks, but responds to a thump.

'That's better.'

I sit down again.

'We went to this – what's it called – Emporium. I had no idea what a hold the Egyptian market had got on the – on the wotsname.'

'You know what? I don't think any of this happened, Mum.'

'It DID happen. I'm telling you.'

'Where was this place, then?'

'In South London. And it was full of Japanese things. Were they Japanese?'

'Oriental, perhaps?'

'Yes – Oriental. This girl who took us was literate all right, but she couldn't speak Greek. Very exhausting. And we didn't get back till lunchtime so I haven't had any dinner.'

'None of this happened, Mum.'

'It DID happen. Don't interfere with my life.'

'SOMEBODY HELP ME! MUM! I DON'T KNOW WHERE TO GO!'

'She's with a no-no little boy. That one opposite.'

'I didn't think there were any children here.'

'Oh there are. On the council estate. Round the corner. But it was unbelievable to me – to be taken to that huge place. It was very interesting. Beautifully arranged. But I thought, "For goodness sake, let's get back home; back to normality."'

'IS IT MINE? IT'S NOT MINE. IS IT YOURS? NO.'

'Oh I went a long, long way. No roads that I knew anything about.'

'ALL RIGHT, DARLING. ALL RIGHT.'

Mother smiles at me and straightens up in her chair.

'You know, I think you'll find that I'm getting on quite well with the neighbours opposite.'

'HELP ME! HELP ME! BERYL! MUM! WHERE ARE THEY? I HAVEN'T THE FAINTEST IDEA.'

I think it's time to go home. Back to normality.

## They Don't Come When You Ring (2008)

Tonight is Bonfire Night. As I walk through the hall and down the long passageway of the care home Lisa calls after me, 'Are you coming to the fireworks later, Judy?'

I might stay. They make an effort to keep the residents amused here. It's a good thing.

'I might,' I call over my shoulder.

When I get to Mother's room, she is in disarray. Her bed is not made, and she is sitting in her armchair banging an empty glass on the little table in front of her.

'Oh, it's you,' she says, stopping the banging. 'Where've you been? I haven't seen you for months.'

'I came the day before yesterday,' I say wearily, taking the glass from her hands and putting it on the window-ledge. 'Tell me what's been going on,' I say, pulling the spare chair up and sitting as close to her as possible, so that she can hear.

'Have you made it up with wotsisname?' she asks, without preamble.

'Who's wotsisname?'

'YOU know!'

'I don't.'

'What I want to know is – where did you spend last night?'

'At home.'

'Mmmmm.'

She turns in her chair, and feels with her left arm for the glass on the window-ledge.

'Where's it gone?'

'You don't want it.'

'Yes, I do. It's the only way to get them to notice you. I need some more water.'

I don't see the logic. Was she banging to get attention? I get up and lift her water jug from the chest of drawers. It is empty. My mother seems to be drinking an unconscionable amount of water these days.

'Mother, you know you only need to ring the bell if you want something.'

I put the jug back on the chest and return to her chair.

'Oh, they never answer,' my mother says crossly. 'They never answer the bell. It doesn't work. Hasn't worked for ages.'

I move across to her bed, pick up the end of the bell-push and walk over with it. Then I place it in her hands, stretching the flex as far as it will go.

'What's this?' she says, feeling it.

'The bell,' I say. 'Just push it. Push on that end. No, *that* bit there.'

Between us we manage to press the bell. Instantly a loud buzzing starts.

'What's that noise?' she says.

I walk to her door, and stand outside in the corridor, looking up at the light above the door jamb. It is flashing. I go back into the room, and sit down next to her again.

'The noise is your bell, which *does* work,' I say, taking it from her hands.

There is a scurrying along the corridor and Mother's chief carer, Dee, runs into the room.

'Sorry, Dee,' I say. 'I was trying to show Mummy that her bell works. She insists it doesn't, and never has. We don't need you, though it's nice to see you can get here so quickly.'

But Dee is laughing. She moves to the fitting on the wall and resets the bell. The buzzing and flashing stop.

'Your mum doesn't know how to use the bell, Judy,' she

says, turning round to us. 'We've shown her, but she still wants to do it her way.'

'What way's that?'

Dee takes the bell-push from my hands, and kneels in front of Mother. She gives it to her.

'Muriel,' she says. 'Show us how the bell works.'

Mother grasps the end, holds it to her mouth, and bellows. 'Hello? Hello?' she cries into the bell-push. 'Hello? Hello?'

She lays it down in her lap.

'No reply, you see?'

Dee and I are both laughing now.

'We couldn't believe it when we saw her,' she says. She takes the bell from Mother's hands and sits on the end of the bed with it.

'She was like this with it. Calling into it. "Hello? Hello?" she was going. "Hello? Hello?" – like that. Oh we had to laugh.'

'There you are,' says Mother, who has been watching her closely. 'She's not getting an answer either.'

This is too much for Dee – and for me too.

'I don't know what the joke is,' says Mother plaintively.

Dee collects herself, and Mother's empty jug, and goes to the door.

'Coming to the fireworks then, Judy?' she asks.

'Perhaps,' I say, as she goes.

'They're setting off some fireworks soon,' I say to Mother.

'Five? Not six?' she asks.

'FIREWORKS! It's Bonfire Night. There's a party going on.'

'What night?'

I lean back in the chair, exhausted.

'Never mind. Just tell me what's been going on.'

Mother reaches out for the glass on the window-ledge again, placing it upside-down on the table in front of her.

'Someone sitting in this chair committed suicide last week,' she says.

A child's face appears round the door. A visitor for the Bonfire Night party, no doubt.

'Oh look! There's a nice little boy,' Mother continues, putting her head on one side and smiling at him. She looks at me. 'You see? HE doesn't commit suicide!' she says reasonably.

Outside her window the sky explodes into stars and rockets. The child's face disappears and I hear his footsteps racing up the corridor.

'I can't think why I was in bed when you arrived,' says Mother, fiddling with the glass.

BANG! CRASH! WHIZZ! SPARKLE! A Catherine wheel goes round outside, in the dark – madly shooting out sparks.

'You weren't in bed.'

'I can't hear with this dreadful noise. What did you say?'

'YOU WEREN'T IN BED.'

'The last time you were here you said, "I haven't got any news except about the BBC – silly, isn't it?" And you said I wouldn't want to hear about it and I said no and think now perhaps I do.'

'Mum, I retired eighteen years ago. I don't work with the BBC any more.'

She squints at me.

'Well, what do you do then?'

'Let's talk about something else,' I say.

A rocket soars.

'What? Talk about what?'

'Anything.'

Another Catherine wheel starts spinning on the fence beyond the patio.

'YOU ARE 105 NOW AND YOU WILL BE 106 NEXT JULY.'

'Shh. Keep your voice down.'

# The Birthday Party (2009)

The small parking area outside the home is full of cars. I have to drive round the corner to the farmyard gates where there is a patch of concrete just big enough to park my Micra. Not many people know about it. My secret space.

As I get out of the car I see our MP hurrying up the front path. Polished from head to toe – crinkly gold hair gleaming with gel, shiny white collar, beaming shoes. He carries a large white envelope and sprints up the last bit of the crazy-paved path (how appropriate the approach to the care home is) to the front door, where I see he is expected, as a uniformed member of staff opens the door to him.

Bother that, I am going to have to wait now while they all throng round him.

I trudge to the front door, carrying my flower-basket (*Best Wishes from the Zurich Pensioners' Association on Your 106th Birthday*) and ring both front-door bells, as usual, just to make sure someone hears. I look around me at the trees and the threatening thunder-clouds overhead. They had planned a garden party – but the best-laid plans . . .

As I expected, there is a long wait before I am admitted. The narrow hall is stuffed with people. I squeeze past them into Mother's favourite music room. She is in her usual chair with someone I know sitting on the windowsill next to her. He smiles broadly at me. Hell. What is his name and where have I met him before? Our MP hovers, holding the white envelope. A huge vase of flowers on the coffee table in front of them threatens to overwhelm the scene, together with assorted cards and wrapped gifts.

'Hello, dear. When I saw you come in, I thought, "Mother's dead." I thought I'd died.'

'Hello, Mum. Happy birthday. Of course you're not dead.'

'How are *you*?' says the chap on the windowsill, smiling at me, 'Long time no see. What are you doing here?'

I need time. Who is he? Denis. Denis something.

'Muriel's my mum, Denis. I could ask you the same question.'

Oh God. I've just noticed the gold chain round his neck.

'Good heavens! *You* are Mr Mayor! We knew you were coming, but I didn't realise you were him. He. You know what I mean.'

Where on earth have we met him before? Before he was mayor. Nice man. Wherever it was I liked him. Denis. But Denis who?

'Hi, Greg,' I say to the MP. 'Remember me?'

Obviously he doesn't. In any event he is anxious to give Mother the envelope and be on his way.

'I didn't know this was your mum,' says Denis Whoever.

Mother has had her hair done and is wearing her best green trousers with a matching green and white top (Marks & Spencer Classic Collection – purchased by me). They have thrust a thick, black, heavyweight knitted cardigan over this ensemble, since the weather is not as warm as we'd been promised.

Vi is sitting at a distance, looking put-out and cross.

'Can I take a photograph for the *Observer*?' asks a young man in jeans, pushing past us to take up a kneeling position in front of Mother's chair. The mayor and the MP bend forward towards Mother, looking into the camera with their best smiles. Mother stares vaguely as she cannot see where the camera is.

'Thanks,' says the young man. 'Are you the daughter?' he asks me. 'Get in there with your mum and I'll take another.' I crouch next to her and smile insanely into the lens. 'And another!' he calls. Our smiling muscles are now cramping up. Luckily he has finished.

'These flowers are from the Zurich Pensioners' Association,' I manage to say to Mum, pushing the little basket closer to her as I scramble to my feet.

'From where?'

'Can I ask you a few questions about your mother?' asks a young woman at my side.

'This is a telegram from Yvette Cooper, Muriel,' says the MP, handing her his white envelope.

'Lovely. Who is it from?'

I open the envelope for her and read what is printed on the white sheet inside: *'Warmest congratulations on the occasion of your 106th birthday. My best wishes go out to you for a most enjoyable birthday. Signed, The Right Honourable Yvette Cooper MP, Secretary of State for Work & Pensions.'*

'Mmm. Who's she?'

'And there's a card from the Queen, here. On the table.'

'From who?'

'The Queen,' I bellow. 'Her gracious Maj.'

Mother holds the card, peering at it.

'What does it say?'

I lean over her, trying to see it.

'It says, *It gives me great pleasure to send you my sincere congratulations and best wishes on the occasion of your 106th birthday on 27th July, 2009. Elizabeth R.'*

'Mmm. Lovely.'

'It's different from the one she sent for your 105th. Not so nice. She looks a bit grumpy. Tell you what, when *she's* 106 you send her a photograph of *you*.'

Everyone laughs.

The MP shakes Mother by the hand and disappears. Denis whoever-he-is remains, chatting nicely to Mother, who hears some of it.

The young woman at my elbow presses me for more information about Mother's early life. Did she do any voluntary work during the war? Either war? Was she in a munitions factory? No, no and no. She was a schoolgirl in the first war and a mother with two young children in the second. She didn't do anything notable at all in her life. Her biggest achievement is reaching 106.

'I've had a very long life,' I hear Mother telling Denis. 'But it's been quite a dull one.'

We all move into the dining room for the birthday tea, as the rain crashes down. No hope of the garden party. What a pity, the guests murmur. The residents come in one by one and slowly. There is no sense of excitement. This is how very old people celebrate, I realise. No one goes to the table which is heaped with sausage rolls, chicken legs, quiches, pizzas, scotch eggs, salmon-and-cucumber sandwiches, egg-mayonnaise rolls and biscuits. The room is decorated everywhere with balloons. In the centre is a huge cake, white-iced with six pink candles. No one goes near any of the food. They sit at their designated tables. And they stare ahead.

'Two children,' I hear Mother saying somewhere. 'A boy and a girl. Exactly what I ordered.'

'Come on, Muriel. You've got to blow out your candles,' cry the carers, bearing the cake towards her and putting it down in front of her. One of them lights the candles and, after four or five attempts, Mother extinguishes the tiny flames. A wailing chorus of 'Happy Birthday to You' begins uncertainly and ends in a ragged silence.

'Can I get anyone some food?' I say, grabbing a plate and putting a selection of goodies on it. I feel I must get the party started. But they like it this way. Quiet.

'I wish to speak to the cook,' says Mother, clearly and distinctly.

'Who? Joe?' I ask her.

'Yes. Joe. Tell him to come here.'

Joe the cook is summoned and waddles to her side, wiping his hands on his check trousers.

'Who's that?'

'Joe, Mum. The cook. You asked to see him.'

'Oh yes. I wish to thank you for all the cakes you have made me over the years.'

Applause. Joe looks close to tears. He ambles back to the kitchen.

Very slowly the party gets going, as I help the carers to hand out plates. Most of the food is eaten by the carers, the guests, the members of the management team from the home and Vi, who has decided not to join in. She is sitting alone in the large residents' lounge next door.

'Aren't you coming to the party?' I ask her.

'I don't know no one up there,' she says.

'You do. You know Mum and you know me and you know Dee and Lisa—'

'No. I don't know no one.'

The term 'passive aggressive' springs to mind.

'Shall I bring you a plate of food?'

She cheers up.

'Yes. Thanks.'

In the dining room Mother has a large piece of her cake placed before her.

'What's this?'

'It's your birthday cake, Mother.'

'My what?'

'Birthday cake. Yours. Joe made it.'

'Who's Joe?'

Next door Vi polishes off three sandwiches, two sausage rolls, a Scotch egg and a piece of quiche, followed by a slice of birthday cake, all on her own.

And I still can't remember the mayor's surname.

# It's Not Good (2009)

It is more than a week since I visited. I feel guilty as I ring the door bells (ringing them both, as usual, to be sure of an answer). I remember Owl's house in *Winnie-the-Pooh*, and his notice: PLEZ KNOKE IF AN ANSWR IS REQUID. PLEZ RING IF AN ANSWR IS *NOT* REQUID. I require an answer.

And I see crazy Edna through the glass, wandering out of the residents' lounge and towards the door. She's heard the bell and wants to help. Unfortunately the security system is such that if she touches the door-handle, twenty alarms will sound from different places.

I shake my head violently at her as she approaches. She is smiling at me, and nodding, bearing down inexorably. I don't think I can stand the strain. Luckily, a blue-uniformed figure appears behind her, and steers her away, back into the lounge.

The figure carries the uusal bunch of keys on a chain. The figure is Ingrid – newly married and back from her honeymoon (at home, with her three children aged four, seven and nine). A tall girl with a compassionate face and a bad toe. She inserts one of the keys into the lock, smiles at me, and swings the door back, so that I can enter the small hall.

'Hi, how are you?' I say. 'Had a good time?'

'We had a lovely day on the Wednesday, Judy.'

'What was wrong with the rest of the time?'

'Oh, same old, same old.' She shrugs.

I move past her, peering around me for Mum.

'My toe's been dreadful,' says Ingrid.

But I am not listening. A strange, tiny figure, seated at the entrance to the residents' lounge, wearing a striped dressing-gown and a desperate look, is rising from her chair.

'Please, please,' she says. She grabs me. 'I need the loo. Please. Please.'

She is unrecognisable. One side of her face is black and blue. On her forehead is a purple lump the size of a squash ball, from which a palette of colours, yellow to green to indigo, stain her nose, cheeks and neck.

Mummy. She doesn't even know me. She thinks I am one of the carers. Ingrid appears from behind and takes her arm.

'Use the walking-frame, Muriel,' she says.

'What? I need the loo. Please.'

Ingrid puts a lightweight Zimmer frame into her hands, and, with an arm round her waist, propels her out of the room and across the corridor towards the bathrooms.

No other resident notices, or cares. They sit in their chairs around the room, mostly staring blankly. A dominating television set of monstrous size flashes pictures from the bay window. Silently. They have not switched the sound on, for some reason. The residents are unaware and uncomplaining.

Why was Mother not in her usual place, with Vi in the small music room next door? What has happened to her in the week I have not visited?

I sit in the place Mother has vacated, on the small two-seater settee.

As the tea-trolley rumbles in, Carol, the manager, dodges back into her office opposite. She waves at me.

'It's a real shiner, isn't it?' she calls cheerfully. 'We tried to ring you, but we couldn't get you, or something.' She goes into her office, closing the door.

'Cup of tea, Judy?' says Anna, from behind the tea-trolley, as she manhandles the enormous teapot.

'Yes, please. What's happened to Mum?'

'She had a fall, Judy. How do you want this?' She pauses, the teapot poised over a mug.

'Not too milky. When?'

An extremely milky mug of tea is passed to me, and I put it on a small table nearby.

'Hold on a moment. I'll get the report.'

Anna abandons the trolley, leaving the residents looking at it longingly.

'How is everyone?' I say to them.

No reply.

Anna returns with a large book. She sits next to me, turning the pages.

'She did it on the nineteenth,' she announces.

'A week ago!' I say.

'We tried to ring you but we couldn't get through.'

Well, that's funny because I have an Ansaphone. Never mind. If she did it a week ago, then she must be over the worst.

'She's lost a lot of mobility, that's the thing,' says Anna, closing the book. 'We don't want her wandering about on her own any more, so she's got to have help to go to the toilet.'

The last bit of dignity and independence withdrawn, then.

'We're persuading her to use the walking-frame instead of the stick,' says Anna, getting up and leaving me.

The bent figure that is my mother is returning from the bathroom, holding Ingrid's arm. Her tiny body forms an L shape – her lower half at a complete right-angle to her trunk, her head stuck forward like a tortoise.

'Come and sit next to me, Mum,' I say, and together Ingrid and I manoeuvre her down onto the sofa beside me, Ingrid from above and me from my seated position.

I pat her hand.

Anna returns and resumes her tea-trolley duties.

'Cup of tea, Muriel?'

No response.

'DO YOU WANT A CUP OF TEA, MOTHER?'

'What?'

'Just pour it, Anna. I'm sure she'd like one.'

Anna lifts the massive teapot again, pouring steadily into one of the mugs.

'Not too milky,' I say.

Another extremely milky mug of tea is put on the small table next to us, joining mine.

'Can you fill in these forms, Judy?' Anna takes a polythene package of papers from beneath the trolley. 'Just the usual. Date and signature where it says.'

She moves off, going round the room dispensing the pale beige liquid to the grateful occupants.

'You've been a silly girl,' I say to Mother. 'Throwing yourself about. You must stop doing this. What have you done to yourself?'

'I don't know.' She sighs.

'Are you pleased to see me?'

'I don't know.'

Mother reaches for her mug of tea and grasps it, bringing it shakily to her lips.

I feel round her head to her right ear. No piece of plastic. No hearing aid. If I find this vital piece of equipment, perhaps I will be able to make some contact, but suddenly she says, 'I fall, you know.' She stretches out an arm and replaces the mug on the edge of the table, wobbling it into position.

'We all know that. How do you do it?'

'Oh, bustling and bumbling about.'

I find her hearing aid in her dressing-gown pocket and shake it, putting it to my ear. It is whistling and peeping. In working order then – no need for the fiddly process of inserting a new battery.

When I have pushed it into her ear and arranged the business end looped up over and behind, I take a sip of my cold milky tea.

'Why are you so daft?' I ask her.

'I don't know.'

She turns and looks at me. Tiny. Shrunken. Her face looks like an injured macaque monkey.

Mummy.

I read the forms Anna has asked me to sign on Mother's behalf.

Are you satisfied with the entertainments and activities
   provided at the home?

Would you like other activities? (Please state which.)

Do the staff respect you at all times?

Can you choose when to have a bath?

Do you have access to the management for any
   complaints?

Are you satisfied with the way your laundry is done?

Is your bell answered promptly?

I take a pen from my bag and write:

DO THE PEOPLE WHO DEVISE THESE FORMS
HAVE ANY IDEA OF THE STATE PEOPLE ARE IN
BY THE TIME THEY ENTER LONG-TERM
CARE?

## Getting Worse (2009)

The telephone message was worrying. 'Your Mum is back from the hospital and we have put her to bed so she is OK.'

What hospital? Why? What went on while I was on a week's holiday?

I arrive, somewhat breathless, at the front door (roses above it – looks cosy but they need pruning . . .) and barge in as it is opened.

'She's in bed, Judy,' says the gentle Ingrid, as she closes the door behind me. 'She had another fall two days ago. We spoke to your brother, but we left the message for you instead of him by mistake.'

'I'm worried about her,' I say.

'So am I,' she replies. 'It's like being on suicide watch with her, I tell you. And there's only two of us on today . . .'

But I am already pushing down the narrow corridor, past the parked Zimmer frames and the odd tottering resident. I go into Mother's room.

It is not good. A large, unemptied commode takes centre stage, and my mother is sitting on the edge of the bed in her nightie groaning.

I sit next to her and take her hand.

'Go away! Go away!' she screams.

The bump over her eye is still there, but now she has fresh bruising across her chest. The V in her nightgown reveals an expanse of black and purple flesh. Her white legs are exposed and I see her ankles and the calf of her right leg are mottled and abrased. Dried blood clings to the ankle.

She clutches at me. 'Help, help, help!' She indicates the commode.

I manage to get her off the bed and onto it. She sits, swinging her legs – they do not reach the floor.

'Water! Water! Water!'

The jug in the room is empty. Taking it, I run to the kitchen.

'She's in an awful state,' I say, holding the jug under the cold water tap.

Ingrid and an auxiliary are methodically buttering slices of bread. They have their backs to me. It is quiet in the kitchen. A large pan of baked beans simmers on the gas stove. Plates and trays are laid out, mugs are ready with a pool of milk in the bottom of each. The kettle is steaming.

Ingrid turns, a buttered knife in her hand. She looks concerned.

'D'you think we should get the doctor in, Judy?'

'Yes, I jolly well do. Will you ring the surgery?'

I rush back to Mother's room. She is still on the commode, but struggling to get off it.

'Water! Water!'

I get her off the commode and sit her on the bed, trying to swing her bruised legs up and round so that she is able to lean back on the pillows.

'Ow! Ow!'

'Mum, are you in pain?'

'Water! Get me water!' She is in a rage.

I pour water into a glass and she gulps it. She gulps all of it. She hands me back the glass.

'More! More water!'

I take the empty glass and refill it, as Ingrid puts her head round the door. 'Dr Reynolds will come and look at Muriel after surgery, Judy.'

'Well, when is that?'

'Won't be till after seven, she says.'

'Water! Water!'

'I think we should get an ambulance.'

Ingrid is doubtful. 'Do you think so?'

'Well, if you don't think this is an emergency, I do.'


Mother drinks three jugs of water while we wait for the paramedics, who arrive twenty minutes later. I am having to hold her down in the bed to stop her getting out of it.

I try to explain the problems – the lack of mobility, the falling over, the cries for water, the fact that she is blind and fairly deaf – while they check Mother's pulse, blood-pressure, breathing. Her pulse is a steady 60 and her blood-pressure is 160 over 80, which is probably better than mine. But she is still raving and crying.

Quite suddenly she sits bolt upright and the pupils of her eyes move to the side of her head like a Kewpie doll's. They're fixed.

'Muriel. Muriel. Look at my light for me.'

She remains fixed.

'Follow my hand, Muriel.'

She raises an arm towards the window, her eyes still sideways.

'It's permanent!'

'What's permanent, Muriel?'

'It's permanent!'

Bloodstained vomit pours from her mouth and down her nightie. She collapses back into the bed. She loses control of her bowels.

An oxygen mask is clamped to her mouth in an instant as the instincts of the paramedic team kick in.

But half of me thinks, 'No, don't . . .'

She makes a gasping noise, and the mask starts to move in and out.

'She's a tough chicken, this one,' says the medic, cheerfully.

# I Don't Think I'm Going On With This (2009)

It is going to be a long walk to the Bentley ward. This is a strange hospital where the entrance is on Floor 3 and the rest of it on Floors 2 and 1, below. You need to orientate.

In the reception area I study the Location Finder.

Behind me is the shop, full of knitted toys, chocolate, newspapers, flowers and get well cards. Along the corridor to the right are all the Outpatient Clinics and, to the left, the Fracture Clinic.

Visitors, nurses, children and doctors mill about in the space. A patient is seated in her dressing-gown, a plastered leg extended, in a wheelchair just outside the entrance, using a mobile phone and puffing on a fag. The sun gleams fitfully. An ambulance pulls up in the forecourt.

YOU ARE HERE says the Location Finder, displaying an arrow. Where? Why am I no good at map-reading? I could ask at reception, but there is already a queue.

I ascertain that the Bentley ward is on Floor 1 – two floors below. It looks as if it is down the stairs, turn left, then right and keep on walking till morning. I bet it won't be as simple as that.

But it is. The Bentley ward is at the very end of a long corridor – past the children's ward, past the Rudyard Kipling ward, past the Fuller ward, past the trolleys, past the dirty linen, past the women's toilets, past the men's toilets, past the cleaner with the mop and the bucket and – that's it on the right. Bentley Ward, it says. PRESS BUTTON TO OPEN DOOR. PLEASE RESPECT PATIENTS' REST TIME 1.30–2.30 P.M.

The staff nurse on duty says that Mother is refusing her medication and is very confused and 'not interacting' with them. No, they are not sure what caused the strange fit, nor the bloodstained vomit, but I can talk to the doctor later. That's her – right over there in the end bed.

She is a tiny, shrunken figure and her hair stands up straight round her bruised face. She would so hate to look like this if she knew. But she doesn't.

'Hello, Mum.' I take her hand, but it is difficult to kiss her as she is in a cot with restraining rails around.

She looks at me with a half-smile.

'Who are you?'

'I'm your daughter, Mum.'

'Of course you are.'

She pats my hand.

'Can you get me out of here?'

'No, I'm afraid not.'

There is a bout of coughing from the other side of the ward. There are three other elderly ladies arranged neatly in the beds opposite. One has a small knot of visitors, another is asleep; the third is the source of the coughing.

'I suppose they'll let you go to the loo on your own.' She starts trying to scramble out of the bed.

'No, they won't,' I say, putting her legs back firmly under the sheets.

'She hasn't had anything to eat,' says a young nurse, appearing at my elbow, looking at Mother, her head on one side. 'Do you think she would like a creamy yoghurt?'

'We can try,' I say.

'They're a very nice family, here,' says Mother.

'That's good,' I say, as the nurse disappears to find the yoghurt.

'Yes,' she continues. 'There are two nice boys.'

I saw the nice boys as I came in. Both doctors – a quarter her age – serious unlined young faces, white coats, shiny stethoscopes. I should speak to them.

The nurse returns with the yoghurt and starts spooning it into Mother's mouth, and I go to the staff nurse's desk, where the nice boys are sitting, drinking tea and laughing with her.

When I talk to them about Mother, their faces become grave and quiet.

'She has made a Living Will,' I say.

'That might be very useful,' says one. 'Can you bring it in?'

'I'll bring it in tomorrow. I suppose she'll still be here tomorrow?'

'I wouldn't like to say either way,' is the reply. 'At her age . . .'

The nurse comes past with the empty yoghurt carton.

'She ate all that,' she says, smiling. 'That's 300 calories!'

'Problem is, she won't let us do any blood tests,' says one of the nice doctors. 'So we still don't know if she's bleeding internally. We think not. But with all the falls we can't be sure.'

'Will she be able to go back to the care home, or what will happen?'

'She'll be assessed by the Social Services team – but not until we are satisfied with her medical progress.'

'And we aren't,' says the second doctor.

I look at the tiny figure in the bed at the bottom of the ward, next to the window. Things aren't going well for her, obviously. But my mother is indestructible. Surely.

When I get back to her bedside, she has pulled her nightie up round her waist and kicked all the blankets off. I cover her up again.

'You know what?' she says. 'I don't think I'm going on with this.'

'No. Don't you?' I say.

'*You* wouldn't go on with it, would you?'

'No, I jolly well wouldn't.'

I stroke her brow and hold her hand and she feels over my palm and each of my fingers gently, then up my wrist. She lifts her hand, still holding mine, up to my face and strokes my cheek.

'You'd think they'd have some cologne. For my head,' she says, letting go of my hand.

'I'll bring you some tomorrow,' I say. '4711. You remember 4711?'

'Oh good heavens, it doesn't matter about the price,' she says.

'No. 4711. It's a brand.' I get up, preparing to leave.

I kiss the top of her head, leaning over her guard rails.

'I'll see you tomorrow.'

'Hmm. I suppose they'll let *you* out.'

As I leave I see her head, with the hair standing up, turning round fretfully against the pillows – small and distant, at the end of the ward.

## Mummy! Mummy! Let Me Go! (2009)

Today I have taken some trouble with my appearance. It doesn't seem fair to the nice young doctor to keep turning up looking like a bag lady. Because he does have lovely eyes and a wicked smile. On the other hand, I am seventy-three. All the same.

So this morning I have washed my hair and put on something of a co-ordinated outfit, peering in the magnifying mirror to do my make-up and generally prinking myself about a bit. If you make an effort you can still cut it at seventy-three. Or maybe not.

Still, I am feeling fairly good about myself as I press the button to open the door to the ward, and walk in, clutching my box of chocolates.

I spotlight my favourite doctor with my smile as I pass the desk, and look ahead at the line of beds opposite, expecting to see Mother's small head at the far end. No sign.

'Where have you put her?' I ask.

'Oh, yes, Mrs Miles. We've moved her into the side room,' says a nurse, looking at a sheet on a clipboard. 'She's just round the corner, behind you.'

Where? I turn and see a room with the door half-open and someone I don't know lying in the bed against the wall, linked up to a drip, her head sideways, her mouth gaping open. This person is very old, very sick and making funny noises when she breathes. Mother must be somewhere else.

'Just there,' repeats the nurse, pointing. 'In that room, there.'

I enter. My God. It *is* her. She is semi-conscious and the funny noise she makes when she breathes is alarming. She has shrunk. She is no longer present.

Someone has switched on a radio channel on a contraption above her head, where a television screen displays the words, 'Do you have any questions? Always ask.'

*Now a trip down memory lane*, twitters the radio faintly.

I lay my box of luxury chocolates on the window-ledge as two nurses enter with a can of drink with a straw projecting from it.

'I don't like to wake her,' I say to them.

'Well, we want her awake,' is the reply. 'We want to get some fluid into her.' They hand me the can. 'Here. You see if she will take it.'

They leave the room, and I gently try to raise her so that I can put the straw in her mouth.

She grunts, and pushes at me with her hand.

'Go away!'

'Mum. It's me. Would you like some of this drink?'

I manage to get the straw into her mouth and she leans over the can, seeming to concentrate on the action of drawing the fluid up it. But nothing happens. She has forgotten how to suck. Or she doesn't have the strength to suck. I try again.

Nothing.

I put the can of drink next to the chocolates and turn back to the bed, trying to take one of her hands. She is still bruised all over and her fingers are purplish. Or is that a circulation problem? Hard to tell. I am not a doctor. Not one of the nice boys.

Her eyes waver towards me. She coughs like an earthquake, deep, shaking and rumbling, and I catch sight of myself in my outfit in the long mirror on the wall at right-angles to the window, sitting on the bed, smart and silly, with her tiny crumpled form beside me. And the box of chocolates on the window-ledge.

'Here we are then. Get a bit of the antibiotic into you, shall we?'

The staff nurse has entered in a whirl of goodwill.

'Not very good, is she?' I say to her, as she starts fiddling with the drip machine, finding its free end and raising Mother's other hand, on the back of which a bright-blue plastic cannula is taped.

'She won't take medication,' she says. 'So we're giving her the antibiotic intravenously. Don't know the results of her chest X-ray yet. She couldn't sit up straight, so I don't think they got a very good picture.'

As she inserts the needle into the bright-blue plastic projection, Mother gives a high, thin scream. She is waving her free arm and her face twists like wire-wool.

'Noooo! No! No!'

'Oh please stop. Please don't do it to her,' I say.

I find I am weeping.

The staff nurse hesitates. She is worried and uncertain. 'It's part of the treatment,' she says.

'No! No! No!'

'Don't give her treatment. She doesn't want treatment. I'm sure she doesn't.'

*Rock with the caveman; roll with the caveman ...* twitters the radio.

The staff nurse withdraws the needle, looking unhappy. I bend over Mother and hold her, while she continues to scream.

'Shhh. Shhh,' I say. 'Don't make such a noise, Mum.'

She clutches at my necklace like an infant, clinging onto it, tugging it, strangling me with the strength of her grasp.

'Mummy! Mummy! Mummy!' she cries.

I hold her close. The staff nurse exits, looking concerned.

*Roll with the caveman ...*

'Mummy! Mummy! Let me. Let me.' She is struggling to

get out of the bed, past the rails that pen her in, still holding onto my necklace.

'Mummy! Mummy!'

'Don't do this to me, Mum,' I sob. 'It isn't fair.'

'Mummy! Mummy! LET ME GO!'

Outside, the nice young doctor looks worried. I speak to him in my co-ordinated outfit, my carefully applied eye make-up streaming down my face, my hair clinging damply to my forehead, my hanky to my nose.

'I don't think you should treat her any more. She doesn't want it. I'm sure she doesn't want it.'

He consults the copy of her Living Will, which he holds in his hands. A small trolley containing library books is pushed past him by a volunteer. Someone is calling for a bedpan. The other young doctor is working at the computer. A nurse puts a paper cup of tea down on the desk beside him.

'The trouble is, the wording is so general,' says the nice young doctor, still looking at the Living Will. 'And we have never had anyone as old as your mother to treat before. We aren't sure what to do.' He looks up. 'We're talking to the senior registrar about her this evening.'

My mother's thin voice penetrates the air. 'Mummy! Mummy! Please let me go!'

'We'll give her something to quieten her down. Is that all right with you?'

Oh please do. For pity's sake do.

# Quiet (2009)

At last she is quiet. Quiet, but still active. She moves her head restlessly on the pillow and her small white, child-like legs move up and down in an endless game of Catch As Catch Can – escaping from the blanket.

Yesterday was dreadful for both of us. I try not to think about it.

The whole ward is quiet today. Nurses walk to and fro on soft-soled shoes, an orderly is mopping the floor in the corridor outside with a soft mop, a trolley carrying library books rolls past on rubber wheels. The occupants of the beds snooze. All the windows are closed. And no birds sing.

I sit by the side of her cage-like bed, the rails firmly raised and fixed in position. I lean over and try to hold her hand.

'We gave her some morphine last night,' says a voice at my elbow, and I look up to see the staff nurse, standing, looking down at the tiny form under the coverlet, as if assessing her condition. 'It's calmed her down a bit. She was keeping everybody awake, you see.'

That's why it's quiet then. They are all exhausted.

'We're just keeping her comfortable now.'

We exchange glances. I know that she knows that I know.

*Thank God it has come.* Keats again. He does spring to mind at times of intense emotion.

The staff nurse turns and goes out of the ward into the reception area beyond the plate-glass partitions. I see her with the nice doctors, bending over the desk and pointing to a sheet of paper in front of them.

Mother moans and tosses her head from side to side. I reach one of her small hands and hold it in mine, which is difficult and uncomfortable as the rail gets in the way.

This hand that washed, scrubbed, cleaned, peeled, chopped and cooked; hung damp washing on the line in the April winds; dusted, swept and cleaned curtains, covers and bedding to the point of insanity – this little hand was always rough and worn when I was a child. Chapped, blistered and ingrained with potato dirt. Frantically she scrubbed at her hands with pumice-stone and nail-brushes, then smothered them in handcream, but they never recovered. She would be really pleased with them today.

I turn her hand over in mine and see that every crease and wrinkle, every crack and line have been erased. This hand is white, soft and plump like a girl's. I can see the other is the same. She is being returned to youth by the hydrating process that is going on under her skin. It explains the smooth white legs.

We are just keeping her comfortable now. That's what they said.

She moans again, her forehead corrugated into a frown. I know that frown.

'*I worry about you so much. Why do you do these things? Why don't you work harder at school? You're never going out wearing that? Why don't you find a nice young man with a proper job, dear? What will happen to you when you're old? You'll be on your own. Who will look after you? Shhh – keep your voice down – don't shout!*'

I squeeze her hand and bend over it so that I can kiss it. Then I lick it all over, pussy-cat fashion, like I used to do when I was a child, for a bit of a joke.

She stops moaning. She relaxes. Her head turns slightly and goes deeper into the pillow. She stops frowning. She sort of smiles.

I think she knows it is me.

I will come again tomorrow.

## End Stage (2009)

The death certificate in my hands is cold and formal: SEX OF DECEASED: FEMALE; CAUSE OF DEATH: END-STAGE DEMENTIA.

I am affronted. Was my mother demented? Odd, frequently, even off with the fairies, but not raving. Except at the end.

'Is there anything else I can do for you?' smiles the Patient Affairs officer, looking into my face across her desk.

She has a small, untidy office, on an upper floor, slowly cooking in the sun. It's like being inside a microwave. Beyond her plate-glass windows I can see the little garden area outside the children's ward below, with its farmyard of plaster animals – goats, pigs, ducks . . . Something is wrong with the scale as the ducks are the same size as the pigs. No matter.

'You must take that to the registrar,' she continues, indicating the certificate. 'And I can tell you now that they only have one appointment available this week – 2 p.m. on Friday. Shall I reserve that for you?'

End-stage dementia, I am thinking.

'Shall I do that for you?' she is asking me again.

'That would be very helpful,' I say at last, gathering up my bag and coat, and manoeuvring myself out of the low imitation-leather chair I am in.

'Fine – I'll do that for you, Mrs Bruce,' she says, reaching for the phone, as I wander out of the door.

'You take care,' she adds.

'You too – and thanks,' I say. I feel like a Speak-Your-Weight Machine. Do I sound like one? Probably.

I wander down the gleaming stairs, smelling disinfectant, watching cleaning staff obsessively mopping the floor below. This hospital was top of the league for MRSA and C Diff infections last year. They are pulling themselves up by their bootstraps.

As I cross the reception floor to the exit doors, pushing past the usual throng of visitors, wheelchaired patients, children, and shoppers who have just popped in for a coffee, I consider the last few days. The doors swing behind me. Cool October air surprises me, sunshine blinds me. Just the sort of day Mummy liked.

She died the way people are born. Fighting, crying – struggling. Screaming for the dark the way babies cry for the light. She had wanted to die for so long ('*although when it comes to it, you don't like it . . .'*). Was she fighting because she *didn't* like it, after all – or was she struggling to get away from life?

How will I ever know? She did not go gentle into that good night – not until her last day. Before that, she kept everyone awake, yelling and talking at the top of her voice. Was she crying out for me? For 'Mummy'? How could I be there for her, in a hospital at two in the morning? Not possible. And yet I feel responsible. Then, it wasn't my fault she went potty. It wasn't. Was it?

She battled to leave the world for three weeks – coughing, tossing, moving her legs up and down, attempting to climb over her rails. She did not deserve to die like that. No one deserves to die like that.

Part of me is amazed she managed it. I feared she would survive to live, bedridden and daft, for another five years or more.

Funny she called me 'Mummy'. She never called her own mother 'Mummy', only 'Mother'. I think she thought she was me, and I was her. Got everything back to front.

My car is sitting in its usual Emergency and Disabled Set-Down Only space. Maximum Stay 20 Minutes. I unlock the door and sit at the wheel, carefully removing my mother's Blue Badge from the windscreen. Shan't be able to use that again – lost Mother and Blue Badge all in one go. I look at my hands on the steering wheel. *'Dear little hands.'* My mother's hands. I look at my reflection in the driving mirror. I have her mouth. I *am* my mother. She thought I was, so I must be. Women all end up like their mothers. So they say.

Will I see her again? The undertaker's said she would be in their Chapel of Rest and we could view her any time before the funeral.

'*Good heavens, dear, whatever you do don't do that. My hair looked dreadful that morning. No question.*'

So that's it, then. Decision made.

Our conversation is finished. Her narrative is over. End of story.

I miss her chatter. Oh God – I miss it.

'*Shhh! Keep your voice down.*'